M000189898

HACKED MINDS

Kat.
Wishing you the best in your upcoming journey. It twas a pleasure meeting you.

Blessings!

Jorge Rudko

7-26-19

HACKED MINDS

A Loss of Personal Freedom

Jorge Rudko

Copyright © 2016, Jorge Rudko

All rights reserved.
No part of this book may be reproduced, scanned,
or distributed in any printed or electronic form
without permission.

First Edition: 2016

Scripture quotations marked (NIV) are taken from the Holy
Bible, New International Version®. NIV®. Copyright ©
1973, 1978, 1984 by International Bible Society. Used by
permission of Zondervan Publishing House.

Designed and typeset by www.greatwriting.org

ISBN: 978-0-9984196-4-0

ISBN	Language	Binding
978-0-9984196-4-0	English	Paperback
978-0-9984196-0-2	English	Hardback
978-0-9984196-3-3	Spanish	Paperback
978-0-9984196-9-5	Spanish	Hardback

Published by J.R. Publishing

*"Dedicated to my wonderful family —
Both the departed loved ones
and those who are still here with us today!"*

December 2016

Jorge Rudko

CONTENTS

APPRECIATIONS

In an engaging and thought-provoking manner, Jorge Rudko succinctly reviews and analyzes features and trends of our modern digital age. His particular strength is to pinpoint, in just a few words, the issues we face, challenging some of our assumptions and alerting us to how our privacy is at risk. He helpfully guides us with commonsense strategies and practices as we endeavor to harness the best of digital power and still avoid the pitfalls associated with it. Read and think about these nine chapters—you will be glad you did—and be sure to share this book with others!
—Jim Holmes, Publishing Consultant

A logical interpretation of the past
A sobering appraisal of the present
A dire vision of the trajectory of technology
A prescription to "unplug"
If you have ever experienced a family gathering in which all sat quietly looking at their electronic devices, this is a book that you need to read. My thanks to Mr. Rudko for his compelling insights!
—Dr. Michael Ruhlen, Medical Doctor

Jorge Rudko's Hacked Minds—a critique of today's overuse of technological devices—is a must read for all people; business leaders utilizing technologies to manage assets including associates, entrepreneurs accessing data in search of their next venture, parents raising tweens and teens, educators charged with shap-

ing young minds, and students who cannot separate from their multiple devices.

First-time author Jorge Rudko displays the literary skills of a seasoned writer. Jorge's conversational style of writing, along with his use of eloquent prose, keeps the subject matter interesting—even for those of us who are not techies. Jorge calls upon great thinkers like Albert Einstein to help support his assertions; and he offers practical, implantable solutions that we all can use to reconnect with each other and ourselves.

I found Hacked Minds to be insightful and meaningful reading — a useful book for anyone who owns so much as a smart phone, desktop, laptop or tablet.

—John Pace, Business Consultant & Social Entrepreneur

I highly recommend that everyone in some type of leadership position needs to urgently read this book. If you want to be effective with the people you lead, you must be aware of an epidemic that will challenge your vision and affect the impact you have on others.

—Sam Rodriguez, Publishing Executive

Hacked Minds by Jorge Rudko addresses the elephant in the room known as modern technology. A fascinating analysis of the effects technology can have on all aspects of the human life. The author has done his homework on the dangers of technology overdose, and the importance of bringing balance in the area of social media back into play. A must read for parents, pastors, teachers, leaders, and students alike.

—Fabian Kalapuch, N.J. District Youth Director

ACKNOWLEDGEMENTS

This enormous undertaking would not have been possible without the continuous encouragement of my amazing wife, Adrianne, who supported and inspired me throughout this lengthy and arduous journey.

I'm also very grateful to my four distinguished sons Jeremy, Steven, David and Michael who always provided an unlimited string of straight views.

To my very good friend Sam Rodriguez, who from the very beginning motivated and taught me the ropes. His contribution was always remarkable and, most certainly priceless, my heartfelt thanks.

A very distinctive recognition to Ruth Chodniewicz, Steve Benson, John Creech, Graciela and Joel Stankiewicz, the talented circle of teammates both from the Carolinas Healthcare System and the Charlotte Area Health Education Center who unconditionally provided assistance in order for me to gain clarity and insight.

Thank you, likewise, Carl Dobrowolski, for your genuine support, wisdom and unparalleled optimism.

Words cannot express my appreciation to my copy editor, Jim Holmes, for all his professional advice and the countless hours of assistance in polishing the manuscript.

Many thanks to Bill Giarratana for designing a great cover and for offering plenty of valuable tips and great reflections.

My most sincere appreciation to my son Jeremy for the countless times that his creativity and artistic abilities were able to dissolve many of the challenges encountered along the way.

Last and not least: I beg forgiveness of all those who have been with me over the course of this project and whose names I have failed to mention.

FOREWORD

From all points, we are encouraged to foster an ever-growing dependence on digital technology and cyberspace. Industry and thought leaders promise a cornucopia of benefits for all eager cyber-natives. But is this reality or a ruse?

We are just now beginning to awaken to the social, psychological and spiritual fractures developing from these supposed benefits. Even during the election cycle of 2016, we witnessed, on a grand scale, what the negative application of technology through the malevolent practice of hacking could bring.

Hacked Minds, containing prescience and caution, warns about the unintended (or even intended) consequences of reliance and dependency on the cyber-world. Far from scaremongering, *Hacked Minds* does not claim the sky is falling. It is not—just yet. It is a positive book with many helpful suggestions to protect the mind and souls of those we love from being hacked.

But that does not mean storm clouds aren't brewing. They are. Readers of *Hacked Minds* will be able to navigate perceived dangers and return to a safe state of equilibrium. Additionally, they will find the freedom as well as the joy of unplugging and mastering technology, before it masters them.

We live in exciting times, in an unparalleled digital age that promises so many advances to society and individuals. However, have we paused to consider the downside, even dangers, inherent within the coming digital utopia? Jorge Rudko does us an immense service in issuing a direct and chilling caution about potentially losing our spiritual and mental freedom. Disregard this challenge at your own peril.

So, be stunned and challenged by *Hacked Minds*. Give it a good think. Take a technology fast. Discuss it among your friends. Pray. You will realize, perhaps to your surprise, that the investment in yourself and others has already begun to enrich you by having read *Hacked Minds*.

—Carl Dobrowolski
Founder & CEO of Goodwill Rights Management,
Brooklyn, NY, USA

1

THE REALITY
OF MODERN
TECHNOLOGY

Tarnishing the Natural Landscape

As I travel from city to city, I cannot help but notice the obvious. It is happening indoors and outdoors—under the same roof, in the same car, in schools and universities, at the airport, in buses, on cruise ships and in planes, at the beach and on the mountains, in grocery stores and sports arenas, in hallways and in open fields, at the dinner table and in restaurants, even churches—and every other imaginable place on this techno-saturated planet. People are transforming themselves into workstations.

With modern computer technology, satellites, GPS devices, biometric and smart cards, you and I can be tracked to within three feet of our location anywhere in the world. Advances in digital technology have made it possible now to engineer an identification system capable of monitoring virtually every human transaction.

Without offering any thought to it, individuals connected to "Big Data"[1] are surrendering all their natural senses. It seems like the need to touch, smell, see, hear or speak is vanishing, and the eradication of all human interaction is rapidly taking place. We are exchanging our minds for the promise of endless convenience and unmatched accessibility. As a result, no physical camaraderie is necessary any longer since companionship is insidiously being replaced by the coziness, availability, and superabundance of necessary and oftentimes unnecessary digital connections in *all* aspects of our lives!

I couldn't find a better approach to describe the reality of this love affair with the current technology than the way poet Marshall "Soulful" Jones lays it out in this portion of his relevant rendering *Touchscreen*:

Introducing the new Apple iPerson
complete with multitouch and volume control
doesn't it feel good to touch?
doesn't it feel good to touch?
doesn't it feel good to touch?
my world is so digital
that I have forgotten what that feels like
it used to be hard to connect when friends formed cliques
but it's even more difficult to connect now
that clicks form friends
But who am I to judge?
I face Facebook
more than books face me
hoping to
book face-to-faces
I update my status
420 spaces
to prove that I am still breathing
failure to do this daily
means my whole web wide world would forget that I exist
but with 3,000 friends online
only five I can count in real life
why wouldn't I spend more time in a world where
there are more people that 'like' me
Wouldn't you?[2]

The introduction of so much technology has changed our lives and, in most cases, not for the better. Yes—in a case of an emergency we can connect with someone quickly anywhere in the world, and I can contact my friends and family five thousand miles away with just a few clicks or a simple touch, but at what expense? Are we neglecting the important things in life that are right beside us just because we are continually connected to something? Maybe it is time to step back and take an impartial look at what you and I are already missing.

If you, your parent, your teenager, your spouse or your friend are avoiding family responsibilities, missing work or education, failing to complete work projects or school assignments, ignoring real-life friends, not spending time outdoors, cutting out activities or events just to stay connected a little bit longer, then you or that other person could most likely be having a struggle with using today's technology. So then, the question may well be asked: Are we the master of the technology we use, or is the technology *our* master?

Nowadays we live in a highly digital world where human achievement is often measured solely by our technological progress. But seriously, should our aim be to produce the most substance with the lowest human input, or should it be to give each person a genuine opportunity to be productive and creative with the richness of human ability? What are the benefits and downsides of the newly evolving brain, wired mainly on inanimate microprocessors and unlimited information?

Our daily routine requires us to use the World Wide Web in one way or another. We enthusiastically turn to emails, social media, and chat messengers for day-to-day communications, increasingly more than for face-to-face contact. Not only that, but with the new generation of wireless technology, we can now be connected even when we're on the go!

Urgent or Not Urgent?

This excessive connectivity has created a sense of false urgency where we feel the need to incessantly know what's happening, lest we miss something important. In addition, the web is so vast that it's easy to get lost in the surfing. Who has not found that, when visiting a site, clicking one link leads us to the next, the second to the third, the third to the fourth, and before we know it we've already spent a good portion of our daily life visiting sites that are *not* associated with what we first intended to do? This may happen numerous times throughout our day.

As we establish our personal priorities and guard against technology's intrusion on our values and thought processes, I think we will increasingly discover that the best solutions to many of our biggest problems are also the simplest.

Now, let us take a moment to ponder on what neuroscientists from Harvard University have discovered. This is what the researchers have stated: *"Publishing a comment in a social network such as Facebook produces the same mental satisfaction as having sex or eating a delicious meal."* Their statement implies that the ongoing "tuning up of self" in Facebook, Twitter, and/or other social networks generates a gratification in the brain similar to the one that you experience when you consume an appetizing meal or obtain sexual pleasure.

This intellectual satisfaction from the use of technology is periodically labeled as "mental sweets."[3] So, isn't there reason to think that this digital over consumption of these "sweets" would actually cause the brain to be altered?

The answer seems to be "Yes." In every kind of mental

activity that we experience, there is change in the neurocircuitry — the synapses[4] (that is, in the connection sites of the brain). So, if we choose to spend a lot of time with one activity for a long period of time, our brain wiring and possibly even our brain structure will change over time. If so, this could have massive repercussions on society. However, on the positive side, because our brain is very malleable, there's hope we can change our patterns back!

I personally value scientific analyses and welcome the creative joy of engineering. But I also believe that, as an intelligent society, we must apply wisdom, re-evaluate the problems we've been asking technology to solve, and soberly acknowledge the collateral effects it can have on all our relationships — predominantly in our connection to mankind.

> *"I fear the day that technology will surpass our human interaction."*
> — Albert Einstein

One of the most remarkable quotes made by the greatest influential physicist of the twentieth century drives us today to recognize the irony of a moment in history where while we are making our environment smarter, we are making ourselves gradually dumber.

It is happening! The inevitable hi-tech enticement is making its way into our lives from outer space where thousands of satellites, as they orbit the earth day and night, are relentlessly aiming radio and microwaves at our planet.

Consequently, the unavoidable question is this: What in the "World Wide Web" is their mission? Of course, the most popular answer could be comprised of many "very good deeds"; I understand that part, but what about their ultimate objective? Are they there merely to provide enhanced communication platforms, speeding the processes of business and providing up-to-date weather forecasts? Or do they serve a less innocuous purpose? Is it perhaps the interest of obtaining absolute control as they gather information pertaining to all social actions and/or events far beyond what you and I could ever imagine?

Who are *they*? You might ask. *They* are those finding that today's modern technology is allowing them privileged insight into all of our personal and private information, our personal and business transactions, and, more dangerously, into our minds. This is something that you will discover as you read this book—and you will find that it is taking place now with absolutely no consent.

People have never been consulted in this regard, and yet this development is completely responsible for changing all aspects of our generation. Besides admitting to the benefits of simplifying most human activities, I see a vital but not so pleasant intent—that is the demonstration of an undeniably dominant capability entirely able to provoke a global hi-tech "police invasion" into each of our lives!

In light of new, paradigm-shifting scientific advances, people should be aware of the extent to which their actions and habits may be noted and recorded. The technological challenges of a "marking and tracking system" for humans are being overcome today at an ever-increasing pace and should be warning signs for the serious and meticulous students, particularly for scholars associated with the topics of this book. Modern technology has created a fearless new electronic world without borders.

Despite the cultural pressure to embrace every new digital breakthrough, we must take a hard look at how technology is personally affecting every one of us. If we decide that constant electronic interventions aren't compatible with our principles, perhaps disengaging from our smartphones and/or other devices could be the way to go.

It may be apt to conclude this chapter with a quote by the great philosopher Robert Maynard Pirsig, who states that:

"The way to solve the conflict between human values and technological needs is not to run away from technology. That is impossible. The way to resolve the conflict is to break down the barriers of dualistic thought that prevent a real understanding of what technology is [or rather, should be]... *not an exploitation of nature, but a fusion of nature and the human spirit into a new kind of creation that transcends both."*[5]

In order for this fusion of a technological nature and the human spirit to be done wisely, we must control technology and not allow technology to control us.

Unquestionably, there needs to be a conscious balance.

~

"He who thinks little, errs much."

—Leonardo Da Vinci

~

2

THE TRAP

Is Society Surrendering?

E very now and then, do you feel as if your life has been encircled by a sense of fatigue and defeat?

Did you know that excessive usage of digital devices can cause sleep disorders and depression, and that's why it is extremely important to underline it as a side effect of a psychological condition classified as "Internet addiction"?[6]

Undoubtedly, technology causes people to steadily fix their eyes on a screen and neglect the numerous in-person connections they should be enjoying with others. By having to keep our faces constantly attentive to a display console, we are being deprived of seeing the world around us, and of taking advantage of life's favorable circumstances — those events and occasions that may instill a great deal of knowledge, experience, and satisfaction in our lives.

Many people are constantly checking the status of their Facebook account, composing a quick tweet or texting someone, and then repeating the same action incessantly over and over again.

Our brains are continually exposed to an environment that requires us to do things that we weren't necessarily made for. Lots of people today go to sleep with a laptop, a tablet or a smartphone on their chest, next to them, or under their pillow, and when they wake up, they immediately go online and check to see who wrote on their wall, if what they posted was "liked," or to see all the new tweets; they watch TV news feeds in the corner of a computer screen, while using the rest of the monitor to check emails.

This shows a behavior that is deliberately and relentlessly influenced by technology—and this technology shows no sign of diminishing in its all-pervasive influence. Therefore, in order for us to disengage from our personal devices, it will require a conscious effort not to make us disconnect completely, but to enable us to make good judgments so that we will periodically take a much-needed break.

How Are You Feeling?

From a health perspective, the challenge of multitasking provided by communication technologies—for instance, updating your Facebook status with one hand, while completing a professional assignment with the other—is an inefficient method of getting projects done flawlessly.

This point should definitely get your undivided attention. The distraction produced by having to attend to the abundance of emails and texts results in an IQ drop similar to that of a marijuana smoker.[7] Without doubt—and if allowed to—modern technology could clog your mind and cloud your common sense, all at the same time. And we wonder why we're always forgetting things more often these days.

It is already a well-known fact that social media can decrease your morale. It would seem as if all the users of the most popular networking sites such as Instagram, Facebook, Twitter, and Snapchat among others, are consistently cheerful, always taking vacations in glamorous places with beautiful people, and constantly enjoying great meals and wonderful moments. It would *seem* as if everyone else's life

27

is so great—but yours... not so much.

In addition, the excessive attentiveness to smartphones and laptops causes over-stimulation, anxiety, and stress. That is one of the reasons why so many of us are generally in the quick-to-respond mode, which fundamentally cripples our ability to calm down and relax, an approach that takes a significant toll on our emotional well-being.

Let's take a quick look at the regular events in a contemporary home. Here is a common everyday scenario, one that I would call "An Online Overload." In the kitchen area of a small apartment in the downtown district of an all-American city, there are two active computer screens, each with email capability, instant messaging, online chatting, a web browser, and a set of open files with chapters for an eBook that someone is writing.

Even after disengaging from their devices, family members are still struggling with the effects of the inundation of data, craving the stimulation that comes from the electronic gadgets, failing to enjoy the simple things like the anticipation of dinner, or hearing about how the other family members' day has gone; and forgetting about genuinely focusing on important family matters.

This shows how people can no longer easily appreciate the spontaneous moments that life affords. It's perhaps inevitable that when a major argument arises, one of the parties ends up leaving the room abruptly and gets immersed in the vast world of video games, or drowns him/herself in some type of social media.

It is also quite noticeable that, in our everyday hustle, there is an unmistakable and increasing pressure to respond instantaneously to any social media requests, particularly those that come from Facebook and Twitter.

And, with ongoing online communications activity, emails constantly downloading to our inboxes, and a multitude of sites that are taking the focus away from people's open-minded dreams and interests, the human ability to spot problems and create innovative solutions becomes that much more challenged.

The fact is that, for most people, the online experience leaves them feeling as if they're treading water, an action that removes the opportunity for them to take a fresh look, gain a new perspective, gather renewed energy, and begin to develop *unique* ideas.

There is no doubt that, nowadays, artificial intelligence is finding its way in leaps and bounds into our daily lives through all forms of technology. We are unquestionably becoming top-notch individuals when it comes to using search engines in order to find a world of information—but not very good at remembering much of it anymore.

The continuous usage of technology does not allow us sufficient opportunities to use our own imagination and come up with any original ideas of our own, or to read, absorb, and think with intensity about any material or data that is in front of us because our brains are so overloaded with online activities.

It is becoming increasingly obvious that our new world system has developed an unhealthy culture of bonding (or better said, "bondage") and reliance—a "bond" between people and the prevailing technology and a reliance on it as if we were automatons.

Yet, we don't need statistics to tell us that we are over-attached to our digital gadgets. We already know this to be true—which is probably why you might be reading this book. We just have to remind ourselves time and time again that technology has a switch that can turn the power off, and that only the informed and alert ones among us will perceive when, and how, to use that switch.

The Lure of Social Media

Social media has undeniably become a worldwide compulsion, a force with ample muscle to dissociate people from their real world and daze them into a nonexistent one. This phantom world turns out to be a domain where humans can always find gratifying but often "bogus" attention and validation.

It is a virtual communication means that, when not controlled, transforms itself into a beast that spreads its tentacles out into an accessible and resilient realm where exhibitionism, voyeurism, and/or interaction-seeking behavior, often combined, are constantly reinforced.

People tend to present only the crème de la crème of their lives on social media platforms—where everything associated with them is nothing more or nothing less than a pleasurable, amusing, ecstatic, and seemingly beautiful world—which in turn makes it appear very seductive, and that is the reason why so many are inclined to become a "friend" or a "follower." Also, new technologies such as computer graphics, virtual reality, and robotics may now create an illusion of life when, in reality, there is none.

Even though we may have never described ourselves as "busy-bodies" it's as if we have been given permission to pry and constantly be involved in everyone else's business. We have this urgency to always know what others are up to.

Time and again, we might find ourselves thinking, "Hmm... he looks a little heavier... She looks a little older... Where do they get the money to do that? What in the world is she wearing? If people only knew who they really are... etc." This may not exactly be you, but if it is, you may not be realizing that this type of practice might be making you become someone you really don't want to be.

This type of behavior very well may be leading us to also create "virtual lives" ourselves that we then have to work very hard to maintain, and often realize we can't keep up with in real life. And despite the fact that we have hundreds of "friends" online, when we finally turn our devices off, we feel very isolated and alone, and the need to connect comes back almost immediately as if our devices have an invisible power over us.

It is safe to say that social media has evolved into a perfect place where individuals can be the captain of their own ship, where a sense of total control exists, a place where people won't post everything about themselves but, in selective ways, will only project the image that they long to portray, thus bringing with it a sense of an artificial "self-esteem."

The *desire* for others to see us as we want them to see us, this constant *need* to know what others are doing and the *urgency* to ensure that we are not left out is the *lure* that often keeps us hooked.

Over-Connected

When we are permanently connected, the ability to reset and refocus on the appreciation and gratitude for our lives (and the lives of our loved ones around us) diminishes and an unhealthy feeling of jealousy, envy, and loneliness is often generated. We are continually comparing ourselves and simply "not measuring up" in our virtual lives. This is based on a recent discovery that was made by researchers, who stated that one in three people ended up feeling "not so good" after visiting Facebook,[8] and, at the same time, they felt more disappointed with their own lives.

Certainly, not every interaction with the most popular worldwide network is a negative one, but when over-connected, the prospect of plunging into a social media resentment mode is apt to happen. Is this surprising when

31

one considers the content and emphasis of Facebook posts, as mentioned before, which range from family happiness to vacation destinations, and from body image to the silly number of birthday greetings on a Facebook wall?

Scientifically speaking, the Fear of Missing Out (FOMO) has been recognized as a newly emerging psychological syndrome brought on by the influence of technology.[9]

Nowadays, we are fully aware that social media streams are constantly filled with everything happening all around us, even to the point where we can even see, in real time, the clothes that our "friends" are wearing, the plates of food they are savoring, the places they are visiting, and the life events that they are enjoying. Within this constant flow of activities and notifications, our fear of being left out constantly grows, and at a remarkable pace.

On the other hand, the effect is so severe that in our always-connected global setting, we don't realize that privacy is becoming a nonexistent privilege. What we actually need is to urgently realize that moments of solitude are good and that it is what generally grounds us to the world around us as it provides the invaluable calmness we need. In this way, we are able to individually evaluate our lives and reflect on what is coming from the depths of our very own souls. And the fact is that there is no technology that can replace that!

The "Off" Button

A very important detail to seriously consider is this: In a world where outside noise is being generated more quickly and loudly than ever, the need for peace and quiet becomes more apparent. . . and is more easily overlooked. True solitude and meditation will always require the intentional action of shutting off the constant buzzing—and our screens—completely.

We must consciously make an effort to slow down now, before life flashes right before our very own eyes, and the unavoidable question arises, "Where did the time go?"

The unfiltered and authentic dialogues, along with the true nature of life experiences, need to be put back in their rightful place, simply because they will never otherwise be able to replicate themselves again. Our world is rapidly changing, and life is still but a vapor that appears for a little while and then vanishes away, so we cannot afford to keep ourselves constantly busy staring down at our screens only to realize, at the end of the day, that we have regretfully missed it all.

In today's technological age, online consumption completely displaces personal creativity. In essence, this is because, for the most part, our time is spent in one of the two most relevant categories: absorbing or creating.

Certainly, technology can contribute to creating but, in reality, most of the time we spend interacting with technology is time spent *consuming*, engaging in a diverse set of activities such as browsing the Internet, watching movies, listening to music, playing video games, and, first and foremost, interrelating with social media. We can conclude, then, that we really don't need additional consuming, but what we do need is more creating. This world needs you and me with all our passion, resolution, and our uniquely styled capability to contribute with significance to the society in which we live.

Do you know where the "off" button is on your device? And do you ever use it?

What about You?

Now, if you would like to find out if the aforementioned digital presence is having a negative impact on your everyday life and placing you at risk of becoming overly dependent, then assess your activities and see for yourself if you are characterized by any of the following:

Are you part of the statistics of cell phone users that claim that they could not live a single day without their device?

What about... the studies that indicate that a selected group of phone owners check their devices religiously every few minutes or a few times an hour—would that be you?

Or are you one that checks your phone for messages, alerts, or calls—even when there is no sound or vibration originating from their gadget?

Are you included in the group of U.S. consumers that use mobile devices as a second screen while watching broadcast images on a television set?

Or are you one of the number of cell owners that sleep with their phone next to their bed or under their pillow because they want to make sure they don't miss a single thing?

How often do you deliberately leave your smartphone at home or in your car? Never?

Is there a tool, an instrument, or any other object with which you have developed such an intimate relationship so quickly as you have with your digital device?

Can you function without your phone?

Because we seem to be able to function properly *only* if our phones are on us, people are at high risk of *phubbing* and/or being *phubbed*. This refers to being snubbed or snubbing someone in favor of a mobile phone. This term was created by the combination of the words phone and snubbing and is attributed to a campaign from the Australian McCann Melbourne Company in 2012.[10]

We may reluctantly be realizing that we are placing more attention on what's on our phones than on the important and possibly heartfelt thing that someone right next to us has said or done; and we ourselves may be guilty of phubbing.

It is extremely important that we find a balance, and intentionally take the necessary steps in this round-the-clock digital world. While our very own life is waiting to be lived and enjoyed, we keep on downloading scores of unnecessary apps and find ourselves completely ignoring the need to include, as part of our existence and on a regular basis, the simple action of applying the brakes! When we fail to take such steps, our behavior begins to weaken relationships, and to erode our own free will as well.

In essence, when we know how to power-down technology, we demonstrate a valuable life ability which encompasses numerous benefits. Even though this is becoming a lost art in our ever-connected environment, the most cautious of us can take time to learn the virtue of discipline, put it into action, and begin to live a full life again in every aspect.

Does the way in which you use the Internet affect your life negatively? Have you attempted to cut down your Internet usage?

Now, here are a few points for you to reflect on:

1. We must be alert and remember that "likes" and comments on social media profiles *do* have an emotional impact when it comes to our perceptions of ourselves.
2. Some significant and predictable facts are that the Internet leads people to engage in a more indulgent or impulsive behavior and it makes them less self-aware.
3. Social networking is unquestionably a practical and useful tool, but not always a real and honest communicator, since we can certainly limit all the negative factors that viewers might otherwise see.

4. We must question ourselves as to whether we are over-ly connected and if it would serve us well to use the "off" button a little more often.

Before springing on to the next chapter, take the time to reflect on yourself and make sure you are not inadvertently falling into the "trap" of modern technology and as a consequence unwittingly enslaving yourself to it.

~

"Anxiety weights down the heart,
but a kind word cheers it up."

—Proverbs of King Solomon 12:25 (NIV)

~

3

THE DEPENDENCY

An Addiction that Changes Human Behavior

In 2015 the general public "consumed" about 15.5 hours of media—including TV and Internet—per day[11], in comparison with 1960, when people spent only 5 hours daily using electronic media; that is a 210 percent increase.

If we talked about how much time individuals spend on the Internet (or how many hours they use on similar types of technologies such as smartphones) many of us are experiencing some type of true infatuation—or in more serious cases, an "Internet Addiction," which can be similar to gambling compulsions or drug dependency.

However, it is not necessarily the time spent that might be the problem but *how* we spend it. The total number of hours spent connected do not, by themselves, define whether the person is an addict, as it may be the only means for that person's work. But an individual whose life is consumed by the need to pay attention to the online activity of others—such as incessantly following them on Twitter or Facebook—may be in danger of becoming socially alienated from real people, especially when that person's virtual activities crowd out ordinary day-to-day activities and priorities. So, when does it become a problem?

If you or someone in your household stops coming down to dinner because he or she is too busy online, then that is a problem.

If a student is so engrossed in an online multi-player video game that schoolwork or regular chores remain undone, that is a problem.

If you or your spouse continually stay up to all hours of the night because one of you is surfing the 'net, that is a problem.

If we are so engaged with our digital device or so technologically connected that we miss what's going on in our child's sporting or social event; that is a problem.

If you are hanging out with other people, have your personal device accessible and are constantly attentive to the entire incoming and outgoing digital bustle and losing track of the conversation, that is a problem.

If you are attending a religious service, maybe a wedding, a baptism or a funeral, a conference, a business meeting or any type of educational activity and you realize that you cannot disconnect yourself from your personal gadget for at least one hour, that is a problem.

If you or your companion, while spending time together, take out the cell phone to check it, place it where it can be seen, or if you keep it in your hand, glance at it, use it or check it every time there is a lull in your conversation, that is a problem.

What, then, is your candid answer? Do you have a problem with your cool digital apparatus?

Or do you know of someone who can't leave home without "his or her" smart device and would drive back from any distance to get it?

Dependency

Research suggests that the person's neurotransmitter known as dopamine is actually all about creating a "seeking" behavior. In other words, this brings about a situation that keeps people continually motivated to move through their world with the will to engage and endure. Mental receptors cause us to crave, seek out, and search, this way increasing our general level of arousal and our goal-directed conduct.

The "wanting" system in the body is believed to be driven by opioids; and the "wanting" and dopamine "seeking" systems work together. It is not surprising that information technology and social media sites with their underlying "seeking" and "wanting" drives possess this considerable power—enough to effectively trigger the dopamine system—which in response generates a radical set of challenging behaviors.

People's behavior setbacks can be described as follows:

1. The *necessity for instant gratification*; once the dopamine loop is initiated, the fixed emotional configuration becomes very difficult to break.[12]

2. Naturally, people *anticipate* a reward with more intensity than when they actually get one, and under observation in MRI scans, their brains show significantly higher stimulation and activity. This means they're more driven by what they might find than by the actual information they receive.

3. When people check an email, text, Twitter or Facebook message, they don't know exactly who is contacting them or what they will receive. This is the long-studied reward/punishment mechanism involved in intermittent or variable reinforcement schedules. This feedback system is largely *unpredictable,* and is exactly what stimulates the dopamine structure.

4. Therefore—and this is an interesting consideration—a short text or tweet, which may only be 140 characters or about 30 words, is an ideal number to fire off the dopamine system. This is a method that is most powerfully stimulated when *tiny pieces of information* are

delivered, just enough so as not to be *entirely* satisfying to the recipient, leaving that person wanting more.

On the one hand, there is "real life"; and on the other, there is "social network life." The real life is all around us, yet we are disregarding it more and more often, and for many of us, this is replaced by the "wannabe" life on the screen. Our social network life provides a hiding place where we can inconspicuously be up in everybody's business without anyone ever finding out. We can even flex our "Internet muscles" and engage in conversations or give opinions that otherwise we may not offer so freely.

Without realizing it, at the moment we became a computer-based society, we started to submit ourselves into the hands of an invisible force, which from its very beginning started the process of bringing our lives to a level of dependency—so much so, that this process is making us believe that whenever something technological goes wrong and/or stops functioning, it is rightfully a cause for us to declare it a major personal crisis. So in reality, when your smartphone or one of your favorite electronic devices stops working properly, it silently generates the well-known anxiety disorder condition Nomophobia,[13] which produces nothing more or nothing less than a sensation that affects people's emotions, and where stress and edginess more often than not are blended together.

Here is a quick rundown for you: if you experience anxiety due to the fear of not having access to a mobile phone, or if you are considerably decreasing the number of face-to-face interactions with other people, or if you have a growing inclination towards communication through technologies rather than communication in person, then you may be displaying some of the clinical characteristics of Nomophobia.

Therefore, it is extremely important for us to be aware that any inappropriate use or overuse of technology produces a negative side effect that can eventually generate serious and long-term consequences such as bringing about significant mood changes.

Moreover, technology—beyond the shadow of a doubt—is significantly affecting people's ability to empathize one with another, sometimes preventing or bypassing ordinary person-to-person interactions.

Also, we become so stretched out having to comment, congratulate, celebrate, sympathize, commiserate, etc. with all our online friends, we begin to lose all genuine sensitivity. We end up becoming "automatic" and less sincere when in person. What used to be a heartfelt expression becomes a prescribed and unfelt utterance and oftentimes is perceived as such by others. With this in mind, careful and immediate attention should be given to "parental usage" of devices.

Sherry Turkle, director of the Massachusetts Institute of Technology Initiative on Technology and Self, has been studying how parental usage of technology affects children and young adults.

Much of the concern about cell phones, instant messaging and Twitter has previously been focused on how children who continuously use the technology are affected by it. This is of specific concern because developing brains (those of youngsters in particular) are especially at risk as their minds are not mature enough to process so much digital stimulation or information, especially when it comes to prioritizing and practicing self-control.

But parents' routine interactions with such technology—and its effect on their young—is now becoming an equal source of concern to some child-development researchers. After five years and 300 interviews, Dr. Turkle has found that feelings of hurt, jealousy and competition are widespread among children of parents who are glued to their devices.

In her studies,[14] she said, *"Over and over, kids raised the same three examples of feeling hurt and not wanting to show it when their mom or dad would be on their devices instead of paying attention to them: at meals, during pickup after either school or an extracurricular activity, and during sports events."* It is heartbreaking to witness a parent phubbing his/her own child; it happens far too often.

We should be more receptive and endeavor to boost face-to-face interactions as much as we are able to, and which, as we observe people's facial expressions, will make us more genuine and sensitive to them—especially if the "them" happen to be our very own children.

Dependent or Not?

Our dependency on technology can only be fully understood when the object of our obsession is not present. If you try to implement abstinence in the use of digital devices, you will certainly learn that you are far more enslaved to technology than you would have ever imagined. And that simple exercise will definitely reveal the typical nature of a compulsive user.

We will not be able to completely know—if there is, in reality, a possible addiction—until the "substance" is entirely taken away from us. And to truly discover technology's controlling influence on our lives, we must start by turning all our devices off, walk away from them, and have a little taste of how strong the pull is to retreat and turn them back on.

In this specific instance, the "substance" is the World Wide Web, and you can recognize that a person is on his or her way to being potentially diagnosed with Internet Use Disorder,[15] when such an individual is experiencing a condition of continued "preoccupation", which is one of the basic indicators of all the other well-known habits of addictive behavior.

One of the most obvious warning signs is the withdrawal symptoms that come about when the user intends to achieve the previously savored "high" and the Internet is no longer accessible; and the tolerance level acquired is evident by the ever-increasing need to spend more and more time on the Internet. The loss of other interests, the unsuccessful attempts to cut back, and the use of the Internet to improve or escape a gloomy mood all indicate an unhealthy dependency.

It is essential to underline that there is a direct risk associated with excessive use of the Internet because it provides the user with the opportunity to turn the practice into an obsession, neurologically speaking, with the possibility of falling victim to Internet Use Disorder, in essence becoming a hostage.

When people become Internet hostages, certain regions of the mind experience a reduction in, or a complete loss of, their dopamine receptors. This is the sector of the brain system that normally allows us to experience pleasure and incentives, thus the dependency connection.

Also, it is safe to say that almost all (if not all) Internet hostages seem to suffer from Stockholm Syndrome[16]—a psychological phenomenon in which hostages have and express positive feelings toward their captors, often defending or even justifying them.

Certainly, Internet addicts who experience only a lower level of the disorder might argue that their dependence is actually beneficial, since it lets them be more productive professionally. At any hour of the day, that "benefit" allows for lightning-fast responses to work emails, making one a more valuable employee. That argument might hold water to some degree, but when it starts to intrude on one's overall well-being, or when it takes precedence over time with loved ones and time for oneself, it might be, then, the opportune moment for one to take control and begin to question how great the dependence might actually be.

If you or someone you know can identify with what was discussed thus far, it may help to know that Cognitive Behavior Therapy (CBT)[17] might be an effective method to treat Internet Use Disorder. This form of psychotherapy educates people in how to identify the damaging thought and behavior patterns that plague them so, and replace them with healthier, more productive ones. When people with Internet addiction were taught how to apply CBT to their Internet use problems, they reported improved well-being and less of the dependence.

Digital Natives and Digital Immigrants[18]

Obviously, today's young people are growing up with this technology, so humanity is inheriting a new generation whom we know of as *digital natives*. They are absolutely in love with it, they're exceptionally good at it, and they cannot live without it! Now the downside is that there's not so much time for communicating in person, so the concern is that there is no eye contact when there's a dialogue in progress or when people are involved in a conversation and, distinctively, they don't recognize subtle, non-verbal cues.

Then there is the preceding generation, the *digital immigrants*; this is the crowd who is arriving more reluctantly. With them, there is maybe a little more face-to-face time, maybe a little less Facebook-to-Facebook time.

Consequently, since brains are wired differently, this new state creates a mental breach, which can rationally be branded as a *brain gap*[19]. Therefore, the challenge for both groups—the natives and the immigrants—is to bridge the brain gap by attempting to upgrade the technological skills of *digital immigrants* and assist *digital natives* with their face-to-face human contact skills.

For some reason, it's more complicated for the natives to pick up on the face-to-face skills than it is for the immigrants to pick up on the technological skills. The immigrants become pros in no time at all! So, being overloaded with technology is not limited to a particular generation any longer. We all become dependent on it!

Despite the cultural pressure to embrace every innovative digital breakthrough, you should take a hard look at how modern technology has been affecting your life personally and those that are surrounding you; if you have discerned that the constant automated intrusions aren't compatible with your personal values, maybe it's time for you to take advantage of this distinct opportunity and make a personal statement by expressing and redefining your very own choices and respective destiny.

Did you ever try to momentarily abandon your smartphone? Perhaps taking a "Technology Sabbatical" may not be such a bad idea.

When was the last time that you were able to disconnect yourself from the seductive grip, irresistible impulse, and energy-depleting power of this invisible force's intrusive aggressiveness?

When was the last time you broke loose from its claws, looked around, up into the skies and down onto the ground, and allowed your mind to execute its marvelous ability to create and release a new dose of fresh and innovative ideas thinking freely and dreaming again?

When was the last time that you had the opportunity to regain your independence from the digital elements that so subtly control and direct your mind every single moment of your precious and inconspicuously passing life?

How Free Are We?

To wonder is a wonderful thing! No pun intended. But, do we even do it anymore? Webster's dictionary defines wonder as: "a cause of astonishment or admiration." It is an "art" of the brain that is slowly being lost.

Now consider the following scenarios and decide whose brain can still wonder. Is it the guy in the middle of a place where technology hasn't made any inroads yet, or is it the cosmopolitan gal who, with just a soft and effortless touch, makes all things instantly obtainable 24/7 at any given moment?

Think for a moment; are your limits of discovery and originality dictated only by what is digitally accessible and programmed into your brain or can you, by personal choice, create opportunities where your brain on its own determines what else can be applied in order to enrich your ideal world?

Are we perhaps becoming the digitally induced retainers of ideas and methods of a new world order?

In comparison with all preceding human civilization ages, we cannot deny that this new era, with the integration of the "information age,"[20] has surely marked the beginning of a most inconspicuous "battle for the mind." This is a subtle reality that gets stronger with every passing second!

Nowadays, without people's consent this digital enticement is modifying our brains and is found almost everywhere! Our minds are very sensitive to any kind of stimulation. So, think about what is really happening. Add it all up—TVs, cell phones, laptops, cameras, computers, video games, you name it—these items are persistently stimulating our brains. Without a single doubt, that sort of exposure is actually affecting the neurocircuitry of our intellect, altering the structure of our brains![21]

47

Take a deep breath and ask yourself the following questions:

Do you get up from the dinner table as soon as your "personal digital assistant" releases a sound?

Do you stay up late, surfing the Internet? (If you are taking away from your sleeping time to be on any of your personal gadgets, your well-being will suffer.)

Do you check your digital aide the minute you wake up in the morning?

Do you inspect your smart device for something you may have missed immediately before and after most events or situations, whether personal or otherwise?

Do you go online while you drive?

Yes, you may think that making use of your commute time to do business over the phone could be considered great time management. But how do you feel when you arrive at your final destination?

Do you find yourself already frazzled before the day even starts? And worse, is your business really worth placing your life and those of others at risk?

Why not try turning your phone off during your commute and listen to something uplifting or educational? Your day may actually go better for you.

Or what about applying a much healthier exercise, like providing your brain with time to relax and rejuvenate itself instead?

In fact, if you use your traveling time to get some inspiration for improving your spiritual and physical health as well as to reflect on your family, friends, and business relationships, you'll notice that the quality of your social life may begin to improve as well, in light of your decision to consciously dedicate time to enrich your mind instead of overloading it.

Why not take a break or set up a computer schedule for

you and your family? Reclaim your loved ones and spend time together playing board games or enjoying outdoor activities, or simply catch up by talking to each other. Certainly you want your loved ones to have memories of fun times together, not of you all being immersed in a sea of digital gadgets.

Isn't it sad to see in restaurant settings, families or friends completely engrossed in the use of their individual digital devices all at the same time, and often no one is talking or interacting with anyone else? Do you find yourself or your family in those types of scenarios?

We all can agree that portable technology is vital in today's world, but it doesn't need to dominate it. Find the balance in your life and make sure you place your family, friends, and your health before your numerous devices.

How did we ever survive without all the technology we have today?

Believe it or not, life was (and it can be) a lot more relaxed and peaceful without the restrictive fusion of the digital age.

Question yourself... How free are you with that need to always be connected? And how free can you really be if you choose to consciously disengage from your devices more often?

~

"He that will not reason is a bigot;
he that cannot reason is a fool;
and he that dares not reason is a slave".

—William Drummond

~

4

THE HIDDEN AGENDA

Coming Soon:
The Threat of a New World Order

While we pay insufficient attention to the obvious, individuals often find that they are gradually becoming encapsulated in an environment that is characterized by electronic sensors to regulate functions and smoothly operate all aspects of our lives. Just as it is with the vehicles we all drive, so it is with our present age, as our society is increasingly being taken over and propelled through a series of automated processes.

Likewise, and evidently with the aid of technology, information has been elevated to astonishing heights. Today, we can actually search online for whatever seizes our interest, regardless of category, and in return, an endless number of links will appear and be at our complete disposal in only a fraction of a second. The vast measure and accessibility of this cascade of data—almost unlimited—is utterly mind-boggling!

Without any difficulty, people are making instant contacts anywhere in the world at any time of the day; emails and texting are undeniably dominating the global interlink scene. Besides this, the presence of media—such as radio, television and the Internet in people's lives—have enabled our entire planet to gather and share—as never before—an unbelievable variety of information.

Moreover, the aid of computer technologies has made it

possible to set in place a worldwide control factor for all buying and selling transactions. A current global whirlwind seems to be rapidly spiraling into a heartless system that one day may likely deny people the right to buy or sell anything, anywhere and at anytime, unless they comply with a common obligatory access code.

Without being asked to grant any form of consent, ordinary people from all over the planet are being gradually and insidiously indoctrinated into a new way of doing things. This new way has no membership class, no orientation workshop, no registration process, no tuition application, no graduation ceremony, and it does not even call for a certificate of attendance. You are not even aware that this is happening!

This modern course is being driven by an autocratic movement that is sweeping the globe. Its intention is to replace old and well-established procedures with a new process, consisting largely in a regimen of powerful electronic protocols.

The endless technological interactivity of our present world is one of the most significant shifts ever to have taken place in the setting of human life!

The dogma of modern technology is made up of a set of approaches that we are taught to believe to be true, that we should be loyal to, and involves the use of programs and strategies that have the power to direct people's behavior and cause them to act or function in certain ways.

Convenience or Control?

Next time you are on the freeway, start paying attention to how "cash" toll tracks are quickly diminishing in number, and how electronic toll collection lanes are rapidly increasing.

There is a present-day event that takes place in the lives

of countless drivers all over the country, and I'm a regular participant of this as I drive from city to city all along the US Eastern Continental corridor. When motorists approach a road toll station and have selected the cash-only lane, here is the typical scenario: cash customers pay the predetermined fee to the attendant, and in many cases they ask for a receipt. Then, as soon as the drivers pull out they encounter a sign that is purposely positioned right after the toll station on the side of the road for everyone to read. The message on the sign states very clearly that cash-lane users are paying an extra sum for using monies as opposed to disbursing the required payment through the electronic system.

These contactless payment devices for fare collection in mass ground transportation systems across the nation, branded as the E-ZPass[22] system, are swiftly becoming the only way to access toll roads and have the capability of tracking us everywhere we go via a radio signal in which an embedded chip delivers our account number, time, and location at various points of the journey. As an E-ZPass-equipped vehicle goes by, the device registers the user's data.

Here is another example of questionable convenience or actual control: Not too long ago, I walked into a multinational cell phone carrier retail outlet to pay my wireless telephone bill. On this occasion, it was convenient for me simply to do the transaction over the counter, and I was pleased to see and talk to a well-mannered retail consultant. However, when it was time for me to take the cash from my wallet to pay the total amount due, to my disbelief, I got an unexpected response from the salesperson saying that there was a small "convenience fee" added to my final payment, which had simply been included because I was using actual currency to pay.

When it comes to effecting cash transactions, people find that their privileges are diminishing. This means that eventually you and I may not be able to execute any business transactions unless we comply with the one and only acceptable government method, a universal access code that will demand an exclusive PIN.

Today's society is being penalized for making payments with real money. It is evident that the right to exercise the ability to use cash liberally is intentionally being taken away from people all around the world.

All right, you could say that tollbooths and retail outlets are not necessarily invading your space. But you can be sure your options are diminishing, that more control is being exercised, and there is a total invasion of privacy going on all around you—and often you may not even realize it!

It was a Sunday evening and, just as I had done hundreds of times before, I was rolling the recycling bin down my 100-foot-long driveway. On this particular occasion, the notice imprinted on it—"Property of the city of Charlotte" (I had seen it countless times)—stood out and seemed to be more eye-catching than ever before. Then I asked myself, "Why is the municipality giving us a free object to be stored in our own property all week long without anybody's approval?" Why can't I buy my own trash can anymore?

Well, after careful research, I learned that the garbage can is not only that, but it's a smart trash bin equipped with sensors and a special Radio Frequency Identification (RFID) chip, able to detect, measure different variables that would determine the type of waste material that I throw in it (in essence, it reads the barcodes of the items tossed in the bin), process the findings, and, in conclusion, assemble all gathered data and be able to transmit it to a base station.

I had just realized that it seems *someone* is interested in tracking what I am purchasing and what I am disposing.

Microchips

Imperceptible and perfectly camouflaged, just like a serpent in his natural habitat; hidden chips that are just about the size of a grain of rice exist everywhere. Silently and undetectably, they store a detailed code, so, when the minuscule 11 mm x 1 mm device is scanned, the chip instantly discharges information about specific matters or common people just like you and me.

When a person carrying a microchip (usually in some form of ID card) is scanned, an assigned identification code is accessed and the corresponding digits will instantly retrieve the person's ID information, medical records, financial statistics, and security data. This may also allow the individual to enter and exit facilities where such scanning is undertaken.

Many people are already experiencing a challenging time getting a job, opening a bank account, applying for Social Security, Medicare or receiving a driver's license, exercising their Second Amendment rights[23], or even taking an airplane flight—unless they can provide a state-issued ID that conforms to federal specifications, which now must include a magnetic strip or an RFID chip.

There are also cutting-edge microchips as thin as the width of a human hair, embedded inside a Printed Circuit Board (PCB). The most significant feature is that it is a contactless interface (no actual contact needs to be made) as it utilizes Near Field Communication (NFC) technology. These are the ones that you wave at gasoline pumps, ATMs, point-of-sale machines, digital signs, automobiles, and industrial equipment.

Similar to embedded chips, some chips can be also attached on the skin, just like a temporary tattoo, unconventionally enabling the linking of the physical realm to the cyber world.

Not too long ago, I was reminded of something I had read about. At a social event that had taken place in two European cities, the same question arose from a particular situation: "Who wants to be bothered by carrying a wallet, a purse or a bag when you're here to dance?" Reference was being made to scantily dressed club-goers who had nowhere to carry purses, and/or wallets and thus were inconvenienced. I recalled that the most ingenious and rapid response was to attach a radio-frequency identification chip to the participant's skin, which, in addition to being very convenient, instantly substituted two of the most absolute and essential items: a photo ID and cash.

Similar to identification chips used in livestock and pets, the human implantable chip already exists and is a syringe-injectable radio frequency ID microchip that can be read from a few feet away by either a hand-held scanner or when the person in whom the chip has been implanted walks through a "portal" scanner.

It doesn't seem so farfetched anymore to think that in the not too far-off future—using implanted microchip technology—whenever a person might want to buy or sell something, he or she will simply be required to wave a hand over a scanning device; this action will read the chip, identify the buyer or seller, and validate or invalidate the sale.

The implant also includes a receiver, which is for obtaining information, and a display for enabling the data to be viewed through the skin. The display is connected to a control chip, and power comes from a small battery. Both of these could be implanted beneath the skin. Implanting is an outpatient procedure, and the battery is rechargeable inductively, by holding the wrist near a charger.

Interestingly, even though a chip doesn't contain any medical records, its 16-digit code can be linked to a database of patient medical information. When the tag is scanned, the number can be quickly cross-referenced to reveal specific medical information about a patient.

On a side note, among many other things that can be done with this type of microchip system is that a signal can be sent from a computer to an implanted microchip-based drug delivery device (different from the ID chip); it's placed in a patient like a Port-A-Cath, and it releases precise doses of medicine to a person and then sends back a message confirming delivery.

Going back to surveillance, popular smartphones, fixed with an embedded NFC Chip, enables companies to store their employee corporate badges and other access-control and ID applications. It can also be used for time and attendance records, network-access control, closed-loop payment at corporate cafeterias, and contactless door-access applications, as well as being able to store credentials so as to secure network-based services.

If we carefully analyze activities that have been highly automated, we can concur that the present order is turning skilled workers into computer-operators, and/or beings that are computer-operated.

As natural human skills are being replaced by automated methods (which technically is hailed as procedure improvement), it brings about an almost blind reliance upon alternatives where one can feel "safe" enough, compromising one's full attention, and "free" enough to divert to an activity that in essence is a distraction. Alarmingly, we have seen too often how these resulting distractions can also have deadly consequences, as when cellphone-wielding drivers and train engineers have caused wrecks.

Giving excessive prominence to information provided by computers (and not using human judgment to double check the work of programs and algorithms) can lead us to events such as major market crashes like the one automated trade that led to the stock market flash crash in 2010[24]. We are obviously caught up in a vicious cycle, which in essence is taking our responsibilities away so we are less able to perform. This is the predictable result of putting too much faith in the world of codes.

Forms of Surveillance

As was mentioned previously, there are various forms of ID processes in the works today; you will notice some are already being used while others haven't been introduced yet.

Another identification approach is the biometric system, which verifies that you are who you say you are, and that is accomplished by measuring and analyzing biological data. This scientific and technological process has the ability to read human body characteristics, such as DNA, fingerprints, eye retinas and irises, voice patterns, facial patterns, and hand measurements.

For instance, during a series of visits to my primary care doctor's office, I had the opportunity of experiencing a progressive but common everyday routine—one where patients were actually using a palm scanner as the medium to check themselves in. This particular device converts the scanned information into a digital form and compares match points with a database that stores the patients' biometric files.

Another method incorporates a microchip that is worn close to the body and includes biosensors that can measure the biological parameters of the physique and send information via RFID technology to a ground station or computer. It also has an antenna that receives signals from GPS satellites, thus pinpointing the location of the wearer. It has the capability to monitor, oversee, locate, track, and trace. It can carry personal identification information and transmit this information through wireless communication with personal computers.

Other forms of monitoring and identification are achieved by specifically analyzing the unique pattern in the iris of the human eye. And there is also a type of technology that translates a person's heat-emitting facial features into an infrared image. There is much interest in this method for use in security checkpoints like airports.

What has just been discussed may seem so far-out there but it's really not. Everything seems to be headed this way, and fast. Simply continue reading and you can be the judge.

Have you noticed those little maze-looking squares on ads, storefronts, flyers, etc.? You are instructed to scan it with your phone and you receive a deciphered message.

A fast data access and a two-dimensional barcode can squeeze in enough information to fit the 272-word Gettysburg Address into an area two inches square and does not require a centralized database. Instead, the symbol itself contains all the necessary information. So should a person ever be required to always carry such a code, all data goes along, in compact form, accessible to anyone equipped with a scanner that can read the symbol. Then, the individual becomes a portable data file, representing, this way, a giant step in component traceability.

Now we have the smart card that looks and acts like a typical bankcard, but because it has a computer chip embedded within, it knows a lot more about you than you may think. Many of our credit cards and bankcards are currently being replaced for ones that have this new chip. It has also replaced food stamps for many, and meal tickets for students in college or employees in the workplace. Soldiers and farmers are presenting them for services and crop reports.

The new driver's license system uses a special camera that stores the photographic image used on the card on a computer as well. Similarly, weight, eye color, and the driver's signature will be stored on a magnetic strip on the card as well as on a computer database.

In many countries around the world today, new passports have been fitted with chips using RFID technology. At borders and customs checkpoints, reader devices detect and read the information stored on the chip, including the person's name, address, and digital photo.

At this point, you can begin to see that with "little brother in your wallet" (or worse, under your skin possibly in the near future), there is no privacy for you anymore. Simply because. . .

- It contains all of your personal information and history from medical files, veteran's status, tax records, your bank balance, to available credit status;
- It has the ability to monitor your every activity;
- It tracks all your financial transactions. Surely, the detailed trail provided in such an identification system is akin to a dream come true for a would-be tyrant.

It is convenient, portable, and it provides immediate access to all the specific aspects of your life. We have been subtly trained to believe this is all a benefit. But ask yourself, how could we have allowed such an invasion of our freedom and privacy? Were we even asked?

We have definitely been lured into a love-hate relationship with automation, computers, and all kinds of apparatuses that do everything for us so that, like robots, we may disengage from tasks that make us stop short of climbing to the next level of our personal potential. In short,

- Embedded chips are meticulously abolishing every-thing we carry around in our wallet today;
- Doctors rely on streamlined, computerized processes to diagnose patients;
- Drivers prefer looking at their GPS instead of street signs (while missing out on the scenery around them);
- Our jobs and the way we interact and function in socie-ty are becoming compromised;
- Our skills are being eroded, leading us to "automation gratification," and blurring our interest in understand-ing the world around us.

And as travelers passing through this world, we have already demonstrated our willingness to accept devices that electronically tag or track us. It has become quite commonplace, for example, for law enforcement agencies to require certain individuals to wear electronic bracelets (and in many cases we can say rightfully so) in order to monitor their activities, but the traveling public have had no choice but to abandon their constitutional rights and indiscriminately be treated like potential dangerous ene-mies of the state, particularly at airports, and be subjected to intrusive bodily searches in exchange for so-perceived safety. Probable cause no longer exists.

Here are a couple of simple questions for you as an in-dividual: To what extent is your life being controlled all for the sake of convenience? Are you being sure to attend to sound information, taking care not to wander off into a realm of myths blindly believing *everything* you are told?

~

*"The empires of the future
are the empires of the mind."*

—Winston Churchill

~

.

5

THE INVASION

An Absolutely
Stripped Society

Through the accumulation and automated analysis of millions of bits of information, everything we do today is very carefully watched!

The fact that active *powers* and *principalities* in today's world may be required to get a warrant to search our "personal digital devices" is of little relief, when they can remotely access a very intimate package containing the "digital me," with far more ease, and where there is much less suspicion of misconduct on their part.

Alarmingly, while we surf, work, and play online, complex and predictive algorithms create a digital montage that reveals far more about who we are than a conventional search of anybody's home would ever reveal.

In the wake of events following the September 11, 2001 attacks, and in the name of "safety and security," the monitoring and tracking of people has become "the norm," and enormous data profiles are being collected on every single person. The United States of America and the United Kingdom, who are evidently leading the way into globalism, have essentially eliminated personal privacy and are now gathering data and tracking citizens in nearly everything they do.

Increased Monitoring of Private Citizens

All civilians' movements and access to most resources are being controlled and we are being severely deprived of certain "constitutional rights." This is exhibited by a silent and systematic behavior, which is continually vindicated in the name of "*safety, security* and the latest fad, *healthcare!*"

If we sought to analyze the clever strategy employed by this "shadow administration" in order to make people accept their offer, what else could be smarter than to conceal and snare them with such so-called life essentials as "Safety, Security, and Healthcare?" Who doesn't want to be safe, or secure, or who wouldn't accept physical preservation?

Just imagine what would happen if we decided to resist submission to any of the proposed items. You and I would undeniably be considered to be people who are totally irrational and, without question, potential "Enemies of the State" and on a global level, enemies of humanity!

If exercising the violation of the Fourth Amendment protection against unreasonable search and seizures continues, and the degradation of naked body scans and enhanced pat-downs in order to travel persists, then what will be next?

Now is a good time to take a look at how civil roles have changed all across the land, including in our own backyard. I remember when I was a child and we were taught that a police officer was one of several public service individuals who were hired "to serve and protect" citizens. When we needed help, we would call, and assistance would immediately arrive; and when protection was requested, we would ask and security would be dispatched promptly. Nowadays, the well-known and original public label has vanished and a new and punitive one has emerged, tagged as "law enforcement." Therefore, today's police department titleholder is no longer the people (who are actually still paying their wages), but unseen *powers* and *principalities*, undeniably the shadow rulers of this world!

Next time you get an opportunity to make a connection with a police officer, preferably someone that you know, or if it happens that you get pulled over (hopefully that would not be the case), watch out for a block-shaped black gadget attached to the officer's iPhone. That's the MORIS device[25], one of many mobile fingerprint and biometric scanners being extensively used in police departments around the country. MORIS is designed to ascertain identity and dig up a possible unpleasant past, but that's not all: the device can also collect iris scans, fingerprints, and photos searchable with face-recognition technology.

Your Footprints are Everywhere
Did you know that your daily activities are monitored in ways you wouldn't even realize, so these details and many more could be open for all to see—and possibly used against you? And that's a problem, even if you happen to trust the authorities to use the data for good.

Every cell phone tower you pass, friend you keep, article you write, site you visit, subject line you type, and package you route through the mail or a carrier—is in the hands of a system whose reach is unlimited but whose safeguards are not.

And if that were not enough and you were not already aware—your Kindle tracks how fast you read!

Everything you do online;

Everything you do on your phone;

Everything you do that involves a financial transaction;

Indeed, pretty much everything you do today is being tracked!

Moreover, consider this: a device may classify a person

as an offender, and that person can't confront the accuser because there is no "physical" accuser. Can it be that acceptable to us that a principle is being established that when a machine says you did something illegal, you are automatically *presumed* guilty?

Public Wi-Fi (a great convenience) raises yet more concerns that none of us would even consider. Routers can pick up your mobile phone signal and are able to triangulate your position accurately enough to determine which supermarket aisle you're in. The way this works is very simple: if the "Media Access Control" (MAC) address of your gadget—a unique identification code for your device, which is visible to a network—can be matched to the user's profile, then whoever has that data will know very intricate details of where you or I, personally, have spent our time.

The point of recognizing all of this is to better understand the consequences of using free services, the ones that rely on monetizing our data via advertising to remain profitable.

Only certain and selected tracking should be permissible in order to target individuals who are already suspected of criminal activity, rather than having universal surveillance through which the private experiences of millions of innocent citizens are recorded and stored.

Surely, if a law, policy, or command were to officially demand that you wear a tracking device, you would undoubtedly refuse it. But there is no need to request it because you are already providing this service of your own free will and they just get a duplicate record of your data!

The same vulnerabilities exploited by intelligence agencies, are similarly exploited by corporations, insurance firms, health providers, even malicious hackers, criminals or terrorists—the very people surveillance is supposed to target.

Do we have a choice anymore, whether everybody gets to spy or nobody gets to spy? Can we choose between security and surveillance? Will it ever be possible to build electronic devices that can only be used for data where such is essential, and abuse may be precluded?

Additionally, "out of control cell growths" commonly identified by the popular culture as sophisticated smartphone applications (apps) are now capable of building up detailed pictures not just of our location, but the context of our environment.

"Digital footprint"[26] is a term for the information we create as we navigate the world, both physically and digitally. This sounds relatively nonthreatening, which is why the term is a poor figure of speech. The true data footprint you leave behind everywhere you go and after practically everything you do is much, much more detailed than a trace in the sand. It's who you are: from your most public persona right down to your most private moments.

Moreover, some mobile phone towers[27] in your vicinity are not always as innocent as they look, and it can be difficult to know how they are really being used. They may not have been set up by your network provider as we all assume, but by the powers of this world—who want to find out who's walking by and what they're up to. Across the US, there's been a scramble for information on exactly what these mysterious towers actually are. There are suggestions that the cell towers are the work of criminal gangs, a surveillance tool by the Government Intelligence Agencies, or even that they belong to foreign spies.

News of these mysterious towers did not come from a research paper or security researcher's blog, as you would normally expect. This news came from a press release for a high-end smartphone!

Fake cell phone towers are definitely an enormous concern. Digital phones automatically connect to the strongest available signal, meaning that it's easy for offenders to gain access to wireless receivers.

Here is an explanation of how a fake cell phone tower can be used to intercept your call: If your phone connects to a fake cell tower, whoever operates the device can listen to your calls, intercept your text messages, and send fake text messages to your phone.

Another interesting fact is that it's also possible to monitor and track the physical location of a mobile phone using a hacked cell tower, meaning that so-called "Interceptor" towers can be used to follow people as they travel in the area of the cell tower.

There are two different types of "Interceptor" devices:

1. IMSI Catchers: These devices collect cell phone information. They can store data for later use.
2. Active GSM Interceptors: A GSM interceptor can act as a "middleman" to intercept cell phone traffic between two devices.

It has been speculated that the "Interceptor" towers are part of a new surveillance network used by the local police force to keep track of citizens and possibly even spy on their phone calls. This isn't an outlandish theory, as American police forces are already known to use "Stingray" technology to track cell phones.[28] These devices mimic cell towers to connect to cell phones and relay their information to the operator of the Stingray device.

Every time there's talk of someone spying on our phone calls, it is usually alleged to be the NSA or another government surveillance institution. This is one of the less plausible theories, although the government already has access to our calls through agreements with carrier networks, wiretaps, and court orders.

The very idea that the most private aspects of our lives

are being monitored by the unknown should make us wary, or at least much more careful about how much of a "footprint" we allow ourselves to leave in the digital environment in which we now find ourselves living.

Right to Privacy? Not Anymore...

Present-day activities show us the intensity of a snowball effect program that is alive and is moving forward without any interruptions:

- Telephone conversations are being recorded;
- Emails are being intercepted and read;
- Tweets and instant messages on social networking sites are being monitored;
- Every online purchase is being logged;
- People's whereabouts are being GPS tracked;
- Surveillance cameras record all our moves.

For instance, here is a striking, present, real-life example. The Florida Turnpike is considered one of the busiest highways in the US and the nation's third most heavily traveled toll road. Not too long ago, I had to drive from Orlando to the busy metropolis of Miami, a stretch of approximately 200 miles. Long before exiting the highway, I noticed that my entire trip was being captured by an overwhelmingly large network of closed-circuit television cameras, which I later discovered are part of the Intelligent Transportation System (ITS). I have also learned that recent governmental activities in the area of ITS—specifically in the United States—is further motivated by an increasing focus on "safety." Many of the proposed ITS systems that also involve scrutiny of roadways 24/7, are a priority of the "Homeland Security Agency."

Now back to my journey—the weather was just perfect,

the road presented the wonderful display of a landscape that was mostly flat, mixed with blue and green colors, and that openly invited me to indulge myself in the splendor of its beauty, which would fade out far on the horizon. In reality, at that moment my single desire was to enjoy the bliss of freedom that was placed right before my eyes; however, the result of a closer examination gave me an identical and very eerie sensation which was so very much like the various encounters that I had when I was in the vicinity of corporate or government restricted areas, particularly penitentiaries and high-risk facilities.

On this journey, I personally counted one surveillance camera for each mile I drove—that's an equivalent of around 200 cameras that were actively monitoring and recording every driver's move, not just my own. And more noteworthy than anything else is that all this, is being done without anybody's consent. Truthfully, at that point I no longer felt like a noble vacationing citizen but more like an unlawful suspect or some kind of a soon-to-be hostage. Interestingly, I began to feel less and less "safe and secure."

As has been mentioned already, we are all very well aware that today, you cannot open a bank account or conduct a commercial transaction without providing "approved" identity documents. These same procedures are also now being extended and applied to the use of different forms of transportation and entry into public events.

Moreover, you cannot simply board an airplane or enter a government facility without being subjected to an invasive search that violates not only the Constitution[29] but also completely disregards people's personal privacy. The Transportation Security Administration (TSA) warns that any "would-be commercial airline passenger" who enters an airport checkpoint and declines to be subjected to "the method of inspection designated by the TSA will not be allowed to fly and also will not be permitted to simply leave the airport."

Of course, the "safety and security" argument made by the TSA in order to advance their unconstitutional program is far more than that. The agenda is rooted in an invisible system of command and control as it expands its duties *over and above* airport security![30] We really should be a bit more concerned that we are being subtly stripped of our privacy, and being treated as common criminals.

Death of Privacy

People's main concern should be that the loss of privacy is clearly making it easier for authorities to implement totalitarian practices, such as the ones that so many individuals have experienced all too much of throughout the twentieth century, seen in exercises that can lead to state-sponsored control and repression.

Until recently, it was difficult to conceive how government or commercial powers could actually have the capability to control the current world population. But now it seems feasible with the assistance of modern technology, which constantly feeds itself with all of the personal data that we inadvertently and unconsciously give. It keeps track of all our movements, and, without our consent, analyzes all acquired information in order to increasingly bombard us with personalized messages.

To have a clear picture of how this as yet unofficial and undeclared world supremacy functions, it is imperative to understand how the hierarchy of nations operates.

It starts with the invisible *power of greed* that emanates directly from the dark world of iniquity to the core existence of the elite or better known as the establishment. This is where the *power of material wealth* resides, fused in an undisclosed command that hides its face behind the labels of corporate settings all around the globe.

From there it goes down to the *power of the law*, which can easily and clearly be tracked down to our institutional government. This is the visible authority that implements the wants of corporate policies. Whether we want to accept it or not, "lobbying" happens, and if you take the time to research how this "influencing" takes place, you will see the connection between the power of greed in many cases, the power of material wealth, and the power of the law.

Subsequently, it trickles down to the *power of speech*; here is the seat of news broadcasting that commonly airs messages to the world population by the channels of mass media through its global communication network. Indisputably nowadays, the influence of communication technologies on human motivation, attention and social interaction is vast, to the point of being immeasurable.

Today, many people—and maybe you are one of them—are utterly exhausted, finding themselves troubled as they witness the hi-tech trend that persistently invades their lives. They have had enough of TV screens imposed before their very faces everywhere they go, and have become sick of the sight of motion sensors, cell towers, microchips, surveillance cameras and magnetic strips everywhere.

I would like to see people exercise their brainpower again and not allow some type of a tyrant alliance put the minds of the masses in neutral and keep them in an idling mode so that the self-centered and insatiable agenda of the elite can be implemented and put in control.

You can be certain that, by and large, people are *not* mentally incompetent in the way that the world system might want us to believe. It deliberately reinforces its contemporary tactics, programming citizens to become docile followers, causing them to remain trapped in the bottomless dependency of a regime that will never propose an alternative for people to stop and back up, should they elect to do so.

Truthfully, people don't need this type of enormous and forceful invasion into their lives. Most individuals are smart enough to know what level of technology is required, and when it is convenient and/or appropriate for their use, and should be able to choose and use such accordingly.

Today, it's important to know that the system's foremost concern is coming directly from the behavior of individuals such as you and me. We are people who still have the capability of using our own wills in order to keep on exercising the privilege of freedom, which in essence defines the so cherished and God-given practice of individualism. We should refuse to submit to a corporate rationalism; this is where the "threat" lies!

Now, the ultimate global monopoly is definitely here, emerging very precipitously and getting ready to control the fundamental right of freedom and privacy. An agenda that is prepared to achieve the ability to command the world population appears to be the most current determined ambition. And many of us are already in a state of unconscious submission, not realizing that every day we are little by little handing over our private information and unintentionally relinquishing our freedom.

Can it be that an unseen force is quickly introducing a technique for the sole purpose of one day making all citizens pledge allegiance to an upcoming global dignitary?

It is now time to realize that our privacy is long gone and we were never even given the chance to say goodbye!

~

*"Those who would give up essential liberty
to purchase a little temporary safety
deserve neither liberty nor safety."*

—Benjamin Franklin

~

6

THE SUPREMACY

Regulating the Inhabitants of the World

Once again, time reveals that what humans have invented can act as a silent vandal of ingenuity, *and what science intended to be a noble instrument ends up being a malicious weapon.*

Behold, a brand new episode in the history of warfare and the World Wide Web: Cyberspace!

Declared recently as the "fifth domain" of military operations, alongside land, sea, air and space, it is the first US man-made military field, requiring an entirely new Pentagon command.

Subject to neither a public debate nor an international dialogue, this military platform has been created in order to conduct a different kind of high-tech war.

At the time of writing, it is said that the computer systems of the United States Department of Defense are searched 250,000 times an hour—up to six million times per day—and that in the midst of those attempting to break in were more than 140 foreign spy organizations intent on penetrating US security networks.[31]

It is evident that in only three short decades, the Internet has grown from the realm of geeks and academics into a vast engine that regulates and influences the global interaction of commerce, politics, society, and, nowadays, even the armed forces.

The increased presence of military, intelligence, and law enforcement agencies in cyberspace is due to the fact that crime, commercial espionage, and warfare have been introduced as three basic threats into our cyber-world. And certainly, a major cyber-attack is capable of shutting down a nation's most critical infrastructure.

The escalated militarization of the Internet is silently demonstrated by the unleashing of state-sponsored cyber-attacks involving the rise of nations against nations, as well as the subtle and not-so-subtle surveillance and censorship of their citizens. Operations such as these are all indications of a world that is rapidly becoming a place characterized by the mining of information, as well as increased espionage.

Moreover, Peter Kelly-Detwiler details in his article in Forbes[32] the possibility of an Electromagnetic Pulse (EMP) attack, the wiping out of a country's entire power grid thus destroying all electronic networks. It is something that could instantly paralyze a nation. A country that is completely dependent on technology could be totally stripped of all power, transportation, banking, commerce, and, worst of all, the ability to communicate. In Detwiler's article you can read an excerpted summary from the 2008 report of the Commission to Assess the Threat to the United States from Electromagnetic Pulse Attack. It is spine chilling!

Therefore, it is important that we be perceptive and recognize that there are significant indications that the struggle for control is on the rise. And modern technology is a key component as well as a key target.

Currently forming, increasingly domineering, and seemingly wickedly motivated, "The New World Order" is rapidly consolidating into a political system in which the state will likely hold total authority over society and seek to control all aspects of public and private life wherever possible.

So next time you hear the word "globalization," understand that is *exactly* what it means. It is the process of transitioning the world system, as we know it today, into a sole global government. It is certainly worth mentioning that the coming authority wouldn't have a suitable platform and be able to emerge if it were not for the existence and operation of modern technology.

As a preview, here are some of today's most powerful world institutions, and they are precisely what they say they are—all components of the forthcoming one-world dominion: The World Bank, The World Court, The World Health Organization, The World Police Force, The World Tax, The World Trade Organization, and so the list goes on.

Whether they are visible organizations, invisible governments, or private parties, they are major Internet players and have "validated" their capability to open and close doors, and have access to the networked environment and its services with all our stored information if they so wish—thanks to all the global agreements being signed today.

Since the beginning of the new millennium, humanity has experienced a continuous increase in the establishing of supremacy in various fields. This includes the development of new tactics that are openly ingenious and yet ominously shadowy. Censorship and data surveillance have become a globally recognized phenomenon, identified primarily in the targeting of individuals in order to regulate them absolutely, though we are led to believe differently.

It is clear that individual citizens are increasingly considered as a potential threat to society even though the vast majority are harmless. So, with that pretext, data surveillance is utilized to estimate the level of *risk* it is thought they may pose.

All around the world, there is no doubt that different forms of control are swelling in scale, scope, and sophistication. This is so, just as much in democratic countries as in authoritarian states. Internet content filtering is definitely escalating, but Internet surveillance—often less noticeable—is becoming even more pervasive and invasive.

The public-private censorship partnerships have produced large-scale structures of control, but at the same time, companies located in democratic countries have been employed by totalitarian governments. One claim asserts that these technologies have been used to track the activities of specific groups and minorities, but it is even possible that such companies have been employed to monitor entire populations.

Evidence shows that dictatorships effectively use the Internet against their citizens. For example, the Chinese government has hired over 20,000 cyber police officers to observe citizens and their use of the 'net. These are "human search engines" that literally go and summon opponents of the regime from their homes to be held liable for what they have said online or what they have looked at. [33]

Now, when establishments desire to extend their control over the Internet, they place greater demands on private sector players to patrol and secure their communications.

Exploiting the Protocols

Now, let us think about our participation and contribution as users of the cyber world. Did you ever ask yourself the question why "a remote someone" is the one that is giving *you* access to *your* own private and personal matters when *you* should be the one and only person responsible for granting admission to *whoever* is interested in acquiring access into *your* private world? And why are we so quick to disclose intimate details about ourselves when, in reality, we don't even know to whom we are offering these privileges?

Don't you feel an "underlying reluctance" when you type in that information? And do you notice that you feel that reluctance less and less each time you have to key it in? Almost like you're being desensitized?

Where is this desensitization coming from, and when was it able to sink into our lives so discreetly that we are treating it today as if it were the new norm? Perhaps, and just like the majority of us, we have simply bought into the "politically correct" and very popular proposal of "safety, security, and healthcare," which very likely is deliberately utilized to strip people of important confidential information.

Surveillance, which is built into the information architecture, paves the way for any powerful party to gain global access to data flows. While the Internet's engineering supports systems of control, it is possible for these very mechanisms to be exploited by the policies of governments and businesses.

The most common form of Internet censorship is filtering. From the point of view of access, users may be restricted by enforced regulations such as: access to the network; access to a particular service (DNS-filtering); access to a specific site (IP-filtering); the opportunity to see certain web-pages (URL-filtering); or filtering based on keywords of content (keyword filtering).

Keep also in mind that intermediaries, like Internet Service Providers (ISPs), can conduct complete monitoring of the activities of Internet users. *You probably never thought of that.* No other online entity has such an all-inclusive view on users' movements so deeply embedded, and, as a result, eavesdropping programs or devices known as packet sniffers can store everything from email messages, to videos, and from pictures to social media updates.

This type of setting enables providers to execute three types of controls: shutdowns, deliberately slowing the connection speed, and the installation of filtering and surveillance systems. Each of these may have profound effects on the users.

The groundwork for control has been created by comprehensive and more efficient data collection and management procedures, which aim at reaching everyone and reaching everywhere. Universal technologies provide all applicable tools to identify, track, and monitor any given person or object, along with his or her communications and activities.

As an example, smartphones aren't just "smart" for our benefit... did you know that by just taking a picture, your precise destination is tracked and recorded with longitudinal time/pinpoint latitudinal precision? "Someone" knows exactly where you are and where you've been at any given moment when you take a picture. Your whereabouts are tracked, recorded and stored.[34]

In this same context, the amount of personalized data not only increases, but also multiplies and opens up more accurate views on users' actual files. In addition, all collected data may become permanently stored, where it is then searchable and accessible, in ways that are beyond the end user's control. And it can certainly be broadcast to an invisible audience, which it already is.[35]

Did you ever wonder how after googling something you immediately begin seeing ads for that particular item or items that are similar? And you thought that was such an interesting coincidence, didn't you? Not so.... Commercial businesses are using these methods to find their new clients. They are hiring companies to track the locals, "see" what cities they are visiting, what they are searching for, what they are purchasing, where they are going next, etc.

Therefore, it is important to understand and to remember that a record of every search action, as well as your location, is permanently stored in the memory of one of the search engines. Even though it may have been completely erased from your personal computer history, you can be sure it is "safely" kept somewhere.

Processing universal data in this way creates even more vulnerabilities. These are systems that do not forgive or forget the darker occasions during the path of someone's life, and they do not have a sense of humor either. Even mistakes, occasional or well-intended amusing information searches, or where a user has scrolled through sensitive issues, can bring about unpleasant surprises by appearing in people's profiles, biographies, or in predictions of their future behavior. This not only is a serious invasion of privacy, but it can also be a very embarrassing one as well.

It can also have practical consequences, since person-related data can control users' access to spaces and services, and can regulate their activities and communications. Person-related data may also be widely impacting on social practices; it can define citizens' positions and benefits, and practically open or close different kinds of life opportunities for them. As such, this ever-present environment is able to create a basis for new kinds of mechanisms of social sorting and discrimination. It is common to hear that potential employers look up social media accounts of their prospective employees before hiring them.

However, going back to the practical consequences, the excessive nature of these controlling capacities goes beyond the dimensions of earlier phases of Internet censorship: these questionable shadow parties may not only get involved in content, but they may control communications and information flows or engage in users' activities and communications through data surveillance and their access to person-related data.

There is an increasing government push for Internet mediators to take the role of controller by investigating, monitoring, and sanctioning users. Operations become blocked, logged, monitored, restricted, and subjected to sanctions imposed by the intermediaries, who fear legal liability for the actions of their clients.

As such, these arrangements would extend forms of surveillance and censorship. They would focus on monitoring all users' data by different types of methods, and at the same time override the borders of users' rights on informational privacy. As these practices become permanent, they may establish structures of control, which can later be used for other purposes—and expand the scale of data surveillance and censorship.

On the Internet and in the Sky

And if all this weren't enough, there is the unmanned aerial vehicle (UAV), commonly known as a drone, which is an aircraft without a human pilot aboard. Its flight is controlled either autonomously by onboard computers or by the remote control of an operator on the ground or in another vehicle.

Deployed without appropriate regulations, drones that are equipped with cameras and facial recognition software, infrared technology, and an audio recording system capable of monitoring personal conversations have the potential to cause unprecedented invasions of our privacy rights. Interconnected drones could enable mass tracking of vehicles and people in diverse locations. Tiny drones could go completely unnoticed while spying through the window of your home, place of worship, school, job, etc.

Again, with very little debate, domestic surveillance drones have already arrived. Law enforcement is greatly expanding its use of domestic drones for surveillance. So, drones are now headed off the battlefield and coming to the headquarters of a law enforcement agency near you!

Overall, the control mechanisms have largely taken over virtual space without a public discussion about implications such as their acceptability, accountability, and social effects. Citizens may not be aware of their existence or understand the altered definitions of misconduct or crime with regard to their existence, since these concepts have become extremely ambiguous.

Now, the safeguards for people are disintegrating, while the domination mechanisms expand, non-transparency and uncontrollability of the major institutions, which hold power (and indeed, developments such as these give these institutions even more control) are highly efficient tools to manage these very citizens.

Civilians may become identified more easily as suspects and even detained in some cases without valid evidence of a crime if their data indicates certain connections. People may also be labeled as guilty, based on the vague evidence of the data associated with them, and so it becomes their responsibility to prove that they are innocent. So basically, the formula may change to "guilty till proven innocent," diminishing the right of "presumption of innocence" established in the 5th and 14th amendments.[36]

However, this ("proving" one's innocence) may not be so easy to do simply because people don't have access to the same extended data that their prosecutors would have. Moreover, the logic of new methods is completely different from that adopted in judicial practices, where a fair court trial should always precede any action such as detention.

People become easier targets of stricter surveillance, because standards used for identification have not only become lower, but have also become nebulous, mysterious, and adaptable, thanks to all the information stored in the cloud. Justification for engaging in rigorous scrutiny does not require the person being observed to have links to any previous crimes, so even peaceful activism and what might be considered to be "abnormal behavior" may lead to increased attention being paid to ordinary individuals.

Information on citizens is stored in numerous databases and registers, which increasingly also cover transactional data on users' activities. The extent of collected data partly relates to the person's own activity and role, technical environment, and his or her activities on the Internet. However, for ordinary users of the Internet, it is almost impossible to regulate what information about them is being harvested, seeing as they are themselves so dependent on the services provided by online networks. Moreover, data collection and monitoring practices in networked environments are largely hidden from sight and highly intertwined.

Most of society is not even aware that this is happening. People don't have control over the "evidence" these networked environments produce themselves. It may be impossible for their statistics to be deleted, and future uses of their data may be uncontrollable. Their files may be merged, manipulated, and interpreted outside of the original contexts for various possible purposes. Basically, rights pertaining to your information may be given contractually to the service provider.

Users cannot safely assume that their records will be fairly used in the long run, since they don't have the means or the right to track or check what kinds of data on them is stored and how it is used. Though it's "circumstantial," it is evident that our data is being used without our consent because of the "not so coincidental" pop-ups we see every day on our screens.

As these practices continue to escalate, we should at least feel somewhat "insecure" and uneasy as we use the Internet for communication purposes to voice our opinions, beliefs, and viewpoints. New regulation mechanisms may one day threaten the benefits of any minorities, or individuals, or groups with different opinions, views or lifestyles in the future New World Order.

So, here is the conclusion of the matter—global control is certainly out of control and the fact is, that there is no place to flee, nor a location to hide; we are completely exposed.

~

"But this is a people plundered and looted,
all of them trapped in pits or hidden away in prisons.
They have become plunder, with no one to rescue them;
they have been made loot, with no one to say,
'Send them back'."

—The Prophet Isaiah 42:22 (NIV)

~

7

THE DOMINANCE

Affecting the Way
People Think

It may seem far-fetched to some, but there is a single, powerful, ultimate force standing ready here and now, to unify nations into one government, one economy, one healthcare, one military, one religion or non-religion, and one society.

In submitting itself to a uniform global mentality, today's society is unwittingly welcoming the arrival of a different type of monarchy, one that is subtly equipped with totalitarian tendencies, and is stealthily making its way into the lives of billions across the globe with the inception of an extremely ingenious and seductively enticing new dominance.

Until recently, in order to achieve such an ambitious undertaking, key components needed to be in place. Therefore, in the latter part of the twentieth century, dominant yet highly attractive technological tools were all introduced to society one after the other. Earliest in order was the television, followed by the personal computer, the Internet, and most recently our smartphones, which have basically become a new appendage to our bodies.

To successfully recruit and effectively alter the mind of multitudes in a nonthreatening way, the primary step was to have a common thread in place, and that first common thread among all the people in the world was nothing other than the launch of TV—an ideal medium. In this way, from its earlier debut into society, it had the ability to consistently and efficiently invade people's lives, particularly their subconscious.

Later, with the advent of the computer and the Internet, citizens were able to learn that television and cyberspace were not contenders with each other, as it had been predicted at one time in the past, but firm associates. Today, reality demonstrates that the two can coexist, play a superior and harmonious role, and converge into a single channel—a channel absolutely capable of engaging a more diverse and larger audience such as no venue or medium could ever have achieved before.

So, it is also important to note that there are methods in existence that aim to translate information into a form that the brain can retain more easily than it could when that information was in its original structure. This technique is recognized as a form of mnemonics[37], known also as digital sigils, and it is being utilized to influence the viewer's intellect. This subtle "mind-hacking" approach is in like manner used in movies, the Internet, video games, and all types of mass media.

Every time you and I sit in front of a TV set, it takes our brain between 30 and 60 seconds to change modes. Before getting all comfortable to watch, the left side of the brain—the part with all the critical thinking skills that keep you alert, awake, and perceptive—transforms itself into what is known in the scientific world as the Alpha Wave State. When this particular mode is activated, the brain relaxes, begins daydreaming, takes on passive learning characteristics, and is immediately set on autopilot.[38] As long as the audience is engrossed watching TV programs, television will relentlessly keep viewers dumb and compliant with its propaganda and indoctrination.

The ongoing manifestation of video pictures that constantly jostle for our attention are actually flickering images that are continually being released from the television set, at a flashing rate of up to 60 frames per second, yet the human eye—which is in sync with its brain interface, and defined as the visual system—can generally process between 10 and 12 separate images per second. Considering that a TV displays interconnected images faster than 12 frames per second, it is evident that the beam isn't noticed because it is too fast to be perceived by the windows of our soul, the eyes.

Another effective method of mind manipulation is through the art of persuasion. In this specific situation, the tactic is to amuse the left brain, which is the analytical and rational side, and to keep it occupied while focusing exclusively on retrieving the right brain, the creative and imaginative lateral.[39] When this takes place, people find that, without even realizing why it is taking place, their opinions and values begin to be modified as they passively watch, listen, and vulnerably pay attention to the media.

In addition to MRI findings on Internet users, people whose brain activities were being analyzed while they were undergoing visual and audio stimulation were found to be experiencing right-brain activity at double the intensity of their left-brain—meaning that such viewers were virtually in a trance for most of the time, and thus receiving their beta-endorphin "dosage."[40]

The reason that people start to feel good almost as soon as they begin to watch transmitted images—and continuously want to come back for more—is because their attention enters the alpha state as the right brain begins to take over. This sort of exposure results in the internal release of the body's own opiates, generating an identical analgesic and addictive effect, which is practically chemically identical to opium, further explaining what was previously discussed in Chapter 3 with regard to the dependency that many are experiencing.

With the astounding present measure of power being implanted by the digital world in peoples' lives, humanity is rapidly moving into an Alpha-Level Society, somewhat eerily similar to the world description by George Orwell in his novel *Nineteen eighty-four*, where easygoing and glassy-eyed people respond obediently to all types of commands.

Consequently, the core question is this: Who would actually be interested in "hacking" the minds of the masses? And who might literally be working to obtain such an all-inclusive dominance? Well, there are currently three active and predominant powers that *may* be extremely interested in accomplishing such a determined endeavor: the media, the government, and/or undisclosed organizations we may not yet be aware of. It is very possible that all three are working in a combined effort.

A very common question will typically form itself into something such as follows: How is all this possibly going to be achieved? Well, unquestionably, this type of dominance is absolutely attainable by utilizing mind-hacking, surveillance, and social engineering.

One might also ask: Why television? Without any further elaboration and as a technological forerunner, television— and streaming today—is certainly the most powerful mind-programming (or better said, "reprogramming") invention in the world, and indisputably its presence is everywhere.

In the Brain or in the Cloud?

Modern technology is intentionally hacking into the way we normally think. Without a doubt, there is a sudden excitement when it comes to capturing instant information, and to have such an astonishing measure of knowledge so conveniently accessible and right at the touch of our finger-tips is breathtaking. However, the adverse situation in this type of practice is that our minds become sluggish and memorize significantly less information than what our brains are naturally wired and equipped to retain.

Every day, more and more people are relying on their "smart" devices in order to have access to, and store their long-term knowledge in, a digital form, which means "up in the cloud" instead of using their own memory. In reality, we are becoming "dumber" as our devices become "smart-er." No offense is intended; rather I'm saying it as a matter of fact, as you will see as you continue reading.

We must keep in mind that our brains use data that is stored in the long-term memory, which is part of the limbic system. The limbic system[41], a section of the intellect that is mostly involved in motivational and emotional behaviors, is an invaluable human asset that facilitates a person's most critical thinking.

If we rely on the Internet to store intelligence—which in reality should be retained as our own personal knowledge, a very meaningful component of our identity—then what we are simply doing is surrendering it into the arms of cy-berspace and consenting with the web to become, in a way, a global prosthesis for our collective memory.

Interestingly, sophisticated scientific methods (involv-ing neuroimaging) have shown that when people are en-gaged in online sessions, brain imaging of frequent Inter-net users displays twice as much activity in the short-term memory as that of sporadic Internet users.[42] What is actu-ally going on is that our brains are learning to disregard information found online (basically, the overload of in-formation floats in our short term memory for a while and most of it is not being stored in the long-term memory).

As a side note, the use of our laptops and/or smartphones in the late evening is precisely where and how technology negatively affects our natural physiological process—the sleep that is so badly needed. As a person's brain works more quickly, its electrical activity surges, and neurons begin to accelerate—and that is exactly the opposite of what should be taking place before we go to sleep.

Another psychological analysis alerts us to the fact that when we are playing a video game, or even simply opening an email, there is a physiological reaction that makes the body tense. When the physique gets stressed, it goes into a "fight or flight" response and as a result, the well-known steroid hormone, cortisol[43]—which is produced by the adrenal gland—is released, and generates a situation that is absolutely *not* conducive to stillness.

Additionally, there is a perpetually present element known as the "glow," (a similar feature to that of sunlight) that radiates from our programmed devices. This glare that looks so insignificant has the capability to penetrate the retina of our eye, reaching into a section of the brain (the hypothalamus) that controls several actions connected to sleep, an activity that delays the release of the sleep-inducing hormone, melatonin.[44]

The aftereffect that follows is that people rest less and less as their internal clock gets readjusted, and that's how the delayed sleep phase syndrome is activated. So, the body cannot physically fall asleep until the new time sets in.

It is a well-known fact that all around the globe, millions upon millions are constantly connected to any of the various digital devices available, either the web, the television, email, a video game, including the almost uncountable array of apps and accessories that go with them. For this reason, take a moment to reflect, be mindful, and consider that modern technology is not logistically, exclusively, and simply there for the sake of entertaining and providing all sorts of assistance to its global audience, but very likely for way much more.

Perhaps, we should deliberately pause and think about it—examine and evaluate our digital surroundings, our out-of-control course, and how all the non-stop bustle is so disturbing to our exceptional existence. Should we decide to change course, we may actually begin to feel the genuine experience of how splendorous life is again, and very likely attain the soul lift that we need so very much.

And here the importance of a wholesome life is captured in a well-illustrated poem by an anonymous author:

> *I wasted an hour one morning beside a mountain stream.*
> *I seized a cloud from the sky above and fashioned myself*
> *a dream.*
> *In the hush of early twilight, far from the haunts of men,*
> *I wasted a summer evening and fashioned my dream*
> *again,*
> *Wasted? Perhaps, people say who have never walked*
> *with God…*
> *When lanes are purple with lilacs or yellow with*
> *goldenrod.*
> *But I have found strength for my labors*
> *In that one short evening hour.*
> *I have found joy and contentment, I have found peace*
> *and power*
> *My dreaming has left me a treasure,*
> *A hope that is strong and true.*
> *From wasted hours I have built my life and found my*
> *faith anew.*

Inevitable Interruptions?

It is completely obvious that the dominance of technology is entirely committed to transforming the consciousness of humankind. Nowadays, we can assert that people live, eat, drink, and die by it. We carry it, go to sleep with it, wake up next to it, and intensively interact with it. It vitalizes our days, and through our devotion appears to invigorate the pace of our present-day living.

One evening, a typical family gathering took place. The table was set, dinner was ready, and we all sat down. Across the room, the television was on and the sound was off, but the captioned images were more than sufficient to keep all present abreast with what was happening. All the smartphones in the room, the digital devices that trespass all civil boundaries, through messages, tweets, and posts, were making their way into our discreet and private assembly. Sound alerts and glowing flashes were repeatedly interrupting our conversational exchanges. It was as if the unspoken thought in the minds of the people at the table was that even the disturbances of uninvited digital guests had to be accommodated, "just in case it was something important."

The next morning, we were all inside a vehicle, on our way to a small cozy breakfast place located in the center of an all-American city. However in this situation, it was the car phone that interrupted our conversation. The loudspeakers took over the setting while one of the passengers, who seemed totally unaware of the effect this was having on the others in the car, kept on talking. So the rest of us started motioning to each other not to speak because we were on speakerphone and linked to a remote voice, which, as is typical, had showed up out of nowhere! So, we kept ourselves quiet until the caller, whom most of us didn't know, completed the delivery of his message and finally hung up.

When we arrived at our destination, sat down for the early meal, once again, there they were, placed on the table just like another set of guests, the "uninvited electronic creatures." When I asked why, I received the same old response: "Just in case, something important comes up and needs to be taken care of."

By nature, human minds are inclined to connect with each other; but modern technology interferes with the optimal natural process, replacing it with the artificial.

Another "interruption", things that commonly dominate in a human and digital device relationship, are the subliminal messages; these are hidden intrusions that only the subconscious perceives. They can be the audio—that is, concealed behind the music—or visual—airbrushed into a picture, flashed on a screen so fast that you don't consciously see them, or cleverly incorporated into a picture or design.

When there is a combination of subliminal messages behind music, subliminal visuals projected on a screen, hypnotically produced visual effects, and sustained musical beats at a daze-inducing pace, what people experience is an extremely effective brainwashing operation.[45] The more time you spend keeping your eyes on the screen, the more your intellect becomes conditioned.

In today's world, the existing media manipulation is beyond belief. The modification of our brains comes from such deceitful tactics, biased data coverage, and false stereotypes. Stop! Think for yourselves! You know what your convictions are, you know how you feel about certain topics, you know what you think about certain matters... don't be so easily swayed.

For your information, when people try to get what they want by unscrupulously maneuvering the sentiments of others, that's called manipulation. Manipulators use charm, good looks, persuasion, trickery, misdirection, and their central idea may be expressed like this: "We have to fool people to make them give us what we want."

Now, when smart digital devices become our idea generators, idea visualizers, sales consultants, directional advocates, friend finders, research helpers, administrative assistants, entertainers, quick communicators, and so much more, what else is there left for us to do?

Stop and think about it; might it be that we are being induced to change the way we do things and, even more serious, are we being dominated and "re-programed" to change even the way we think?

~

"Hold on to instruction,
do not let it go; guard it well,
for it is your life."

— **Proverbs of King Solomon 4:13 (NIV)**

~

8

OUR EVOLUTION THROUGH MODERN TECHNOLOGY

So Where Are We Going?

More than two billion minds worldwide[46] are currently undergoing an unprecedented assault that you and I cannot ignore, one that comes from the excessive influence that results from the accelerated expansion and mundane routine of modern technology, which is imposing itself upon mankind like never before. In today's hi-tech culture lexicon, this phenomenon is defined as big data.

As you have read throughout this book and are now aware, it arrives from numerous sources at an alarming velocity, in large volume, and with immense variety. It is being generated by everything around us at all times, produced by every digital process and social media exchange, and transmitted by an almost infinite number of systems, sensors, and mobile devices.

If we can just hold on a moment, step back into our recent past and quickly survey how technology has evolved, including its impact on the development of social communication, we'll be able to view distinct periods that characterize the most scientifically accelerated decades in world history.

In the 1960s, artificial intelligence was just a newborn; its influence on humanity was minimal, and it was merely a novelty.

In the 1970s it was still a child, but it gradually became integrated into the field of academics, yet with relatively little impact on society.

In the 1980s, still a youngster, it started to make conspicuous inroads into our homes, and led people into a modification of behaviors.

In the 1990s, just like an adolescent, it had some control available but didn't know what to do with it; it was everywhere on the globe, and it began to connect us all.

In the 2000s, it was growing up and felt very vogue about itself, enabling a more unified network of worldwide communications. Its growth turned out to be explosive, and just like most explosions it was unrestrained.

In the 2010s, the electronic brain entered adulthood and became fully integrated into people's daily lives, triggering in each of us the compulsion to be completely engaged in an absolute digital domain.

Today, the clear and unbridled evolution of modern technology, along with the lessening of the competency of the human mind, dominates virtually every facet of our lives—the result—"hacked minds."

Impacting Human Behaviors

The progression of technology incites in each of us a certain set of behaviors—that is, in essence, the expected natural response of our own self. If we are not careful, a disorder that develops from the obsession of that which we become excessively concerned about or focused on can grow into a habit that weakens us, therefore causing harm not only to ourselves but also to those around us.

Consequently, compulsive behavior (the twin sister of obsession)—an unwanted response known as the loss of restraint—will do whatever it takes to gratify preset desires, even though our intellect gives out signals in order to make us aware of actions that could be prevented but which, when ignored, have the potential to generate considerable damage to ourselves. These are behaviors or rituals that you feel driven to act out again and again.

Usually, these compulsive behaviors are performed in an attempt to make obsessions go away. For example, if you didn't take a flattering *selfie* today, you might develop an anxiety for having missed your high at that moment which was so exhilarating for you.

Furthermore, an anxiety disarray characterized by uncontrollable, unwanted thoughts, and repetitive ritualized behaviors that make communities feel compelled to perform, could eventually become known as a *Tech* Obsessive-Compulsive Disorder (OCD). A person with such a conduct would probably recognize that obsessive thoughts and compulsive behaviors are irrational—but even so, that person still would feel unable to resist them and break free.

Just like the appearance of the dreaded spinning pinwheel icon in your personal digital gear, these actions cause the brain to get trapped in a particular thought or urge. For example, you may update your online status twenty times daily to make sure that your "friends" know where you are, whom you are with, and what you are doing; or you ask visitors to like you; or perhaps you surf the Internet for endless hours.

Now, let's make sure it is understood that obsessive habits are involuntary, coming from seemingly uncontrollable thoughts, images, or impulses that occur over and over again in a person's mind. You don't want to have these inclinations but you can't stop them. Unfortunately, obsessive thoughts are often disturbing and distracting.

Moreover, any relief that you may get from acting on your obsessive impulse never lasts. In fact, the obsessive thoughts usually come back, stronger. And the compulsive behaviors often end up causing inadvertent anxiety themselves, as they become more demanding and more time consuming.

The Power of a Digital Imagination

Since the ability to create a mental image, which is also recognized as the power of imagination, does not require the actual contribution of any of our five senses, present-day technology liberally provides us with an ingenious opportunity to shape perceptions for us.

It's imperative for us to understand that the artificial imagination feed can take us to remote and idealistically perfect places at an incredible pace, leading our minds to believe that there are absolutely no obstacles, that there is abundant freedom, and that there is immunity to any worries during that chosen—yet fictional—journey. This can be beneficial as an occasional relaxation technique but detrimental when these "fictional journeys" become so appealing that they begin replacing real life and delaying the need to deal with certain issues.

Under the current cyber age order, we are challenged more than ever before to *renew our minds* on a day-to-day basis in order to take captive every thought, and make each of them submissive to *our own personal values and convictions.*

However, if we continually disregard what is going on as we are immersed in our devices, if we react carelessly and do not take control of the situation, modern technology, which has no empathy or concern for any human feelings, will without doubt define and execute its very own code of ethics for each one of us.

It goes without saying that the power of digital imagination is exceptionally dominant, and, if we let it run wildly, our existence as individuals may not be as unique, exciting, and successful as we would have desired it to be. Therefore, the inability to comprehend what is actually going on may result in feelings of responsibility for the agony, incompetence, difficulties, failures, and despair that we all experience. For example, an insufficient number of responses from our electronic networking initiatives, the lack of new Facebook friends, the absence of sufficient "likes," or the number of people who follow us condition our mind to develop an attitude of accusation toward our own self-identity, thus affecting our destiny.

Nearly three thousand years ago, a very wise king put it relatively well in the first chapter of one of his writings when he said: "Everything is tedious beyond description. No matter how much we see, we are never satisfied and no matter how much we hear, we are never fulfilled."[47]

The promises of contemporary technology always come with some type of a tradeoff—for instance:

- When traveling, the ease with which we use our smartphones makes our worldwide activities simpler and keeps us connected with life back home in exchange for this opportunity of making new and real life connections. So we are less likely to have the impromptu and exhilarating moment we craved for before setting off on the adventure.
- Smart devices promise a map of the entire world in our pockets and a little blue dot that tells us exactly where we are in exchange for the evaporation of spontaneity, and the awe that comes with visual discovery of the scenery that is all around us.
- Technology assures us an instant feed in exchange for the eradication of striking up a face-to-face conversation with a fellow human.

Our intellect is substantially shaped by the actions of our daily life. This is not figuratively or metaphorically speaking, but literally! At a microcellular level, the infinitely complex network of nerve cells that make up the fundamental parts of our brain actually change in response to experiences and stimulations.[48] Therefore, our surroundings and the activities we engage in have a major impact on the way our brain develops and how it is transformed into exceptional human intelligence that generates nothing more and nothing less than a million new connections every second of our lives. And that is just a modest introduction to our intelligence, a natural flexible model that, among many other things, includes the ability to reason, plan, solve problems, think abstractly, comprehend complex ideas, learn quickly, and benefit from experience.

Challenging Human Identity

A downpour of information constantly contests our personal uniqueness. The need to match up to or exceed what others are doing drives us to "create" an image of ourselves (an identity) that is not personal but rather blends in with the rest. This is where the options that a modern-day user encounters must be faced: whether to absorb the entire novel, the electronic way with its challenges and opportunities, or to reject part of it for a more realistic life—one with more of a sense of liberty to simply be content with who we truly are.

Human identity, the idea that defines each and every one of us, could be facing an unprecedented trial. It is a predicament that would threaten long-held notions of who we are, what we do, and how we behave. It goes right to the heart—or the head—of us all. This calamity—a crisis of identity—could reshape how we interact with each other, alter what makes us happy, and modify our capacity for reaching our full potential as individuals. Undeniably, our minds are under threat from the ever-expanding world of digital technology: smartphones, Cloud Computing, Multi-Touch Tablets—and so the list goes on.

Historically, notions of human identity were greatly simpler and quite limited. They were defined by the family we were born into and our position within that household. Social advancement was nearly impossible, and the concept of "individuality" did not exist. That only arrived mainly with the Industrial Revolution,[49] which for the first time offered rewards for initiative, ingenuity, and ambition. Suddenly, people had their own life stories—ones that could be shaped by their own thoughts and actions—spans in time where individuals had a real sense of self.

Nowadays, with our minds under such a widespread assault from everything taking place around us, there's a danger that that cherished self-awareness could be diminished or even lost, particularly when attention spans are becoming shorter, personal communication skills are reduced, and there's a marked reduction in the ability to think in abstract terms.

Our digitally driven community interprets the world through screen-shaped eyes. It's almost as if something hasn't really happened until it's been posted on Facebook, Twitter or Instagram.

Today's technology is already generating a marked shift in the way we think and behave; the love of pleasure is becoming the be-all and end-all of many lives, especially among the young.

History tells us that for some people, gratification meant wine, romance, and song; for others, and more recently, it meant sex, drugs, and rock 'n' roll; and for millions today, it means endless hours of digital interactions on any of the countless digital devices that we all have at our disposal.

Freeing Ourselves

Yet, as we're bombarded with emails, tweets and status updates, it's easy to feel as if we are slaves to the gadgets in our lives. The advantages of being connected are great, but we don't *have* to be trapped in the clutches of unnecessary connectivity.

Our society has become hooked on devices and the social identities we all live out in the digital world. This tangle of excessive connectedness is only getting more complex. In addition to smartphones, tablets have become our couch companions, while laptops and desktop computers rule in our corporate environment. We have now reached the point that people are beginning their journey into this realm at younger and younger ages.

A personal evaluation of our relationship with today's technology would reveal that the more we allow our devices to evolve in our lives, the more we risk isolating ourselves from the actual world. This happens when we turn our eyes away from the physical settings all around us toward the ones playing out on our screens.

In today's environment, it is not uncommon for people to demonstrate a radical shift in their conduct. Here are a few examples to illustrate it:

- A prospective employee has actually answered a phone call or a text message in the middle of a job interview.
- Students in the classroom or parishioners at the place of worship are physically there but their attention is focused on their smartphones.

- Parents are often seemingly absorbed by a smart device, and most of them are evidently focused more on their digital gizmo than on their children. Some even react irritably when their kids interrupt them and ask for their attention.
- Some grown-ups act like the world is coming to an end when they have no connectivity, and they become very anxious when a Wi-Fi signal is not available.

Fear of missing out (FOMO) might drive absorption with devices, but the blurring of our personal, professional, and online lives—and the ease with which we can move between them—has driven our habit. It's almost insane how people's communication skills have plummeted while their technology skills have escalated.

Easy access to them, apparent user anonymity, and their constant availability help us understand some reasons why we can fall so in love with our gadgets. A smartphone is always with you. It acts as a lifeline to friends and family, delivers news from around the globe as well as gossip from your inner circle, and lets you play videos, music, or games when you're bored.

I recall not too long ago I read a sign that included to some extent, the following statement about our modern-day world: "We have turned our land into a nation of *smart* phones and *idiotic* people."

Pretty soon, we could all have devices strapped to our bodies, text messages beamed to our retinas, and sensors telling us we've been in the sun too long, while electronics makers are busy assembling cars, refrigerators, thermostats, luggage, and other smart appliances that talk back to us.

Now, with that frank statement in mind and in order for us to bring consciousness to a world that is losing its

identity, a fundamental blueprint for action would probably be extremely beneficial. So here we go; let's start by
implementing this four-step approach:

1. *Resist the Attraction*
   Be aware how dazzlingly enticing big data and its
   plethora of gadgets can be; and don't give in.
2. *Refuse the Persuasion*
   Be resilient; do not compromise your values or be easily convinced.
3. *Realize the Contamination*
   Be attentive to warning signs (such as an underlying
   reluctance) and don't trade yourself or your loved ones
   in.
4. *Recognize the Regime*
   Be alert to a system that is in place to undermine and to
   seduce you into complacency.

How do you guard your heart?
- Be informed; that's what you did by reading this book.
- Be aware; look around and question, are you contro-
  lling technology or is technology controlling you?
- Take action; make the necessary decisions to change
  what needs to be changed...
- Delete time-consuming or frivolous apps; consciously
  limiting the time spent surfing or on social media
- Disengage from your devices; begin to live "real" life a
  little more each day
- Rediscover; your family, friends, nature, your hobbies,
  talents, and dreams.

**Take back your "hacked mind"
and regain your FREEDOM!**

~

*"Do not conform to the pattern of this world,
but be transformed by the renewing
of your mind."*

— Saint Paul to the Romans 12:2a (NIV))

~

9

BY THE WAY...
IT'S NOT ALL BAD

Utilizing Technology Wisely

I must emphasize and recognize, some of the noteworthy benefits that modern technology offers humanity. Thanks to some significant findings and discoveries, the world has become smaller and more receptive. Were it not for technology, you wouldn't have read this book. From telephones to the Internet, from calculators to computers, and from cars to airplanes and satellites, we are immersed in a sea of discoveries.

Technology has simplified and made our lives easier, all the while bringing amenities never before imagined to people like you and me.

Information technology, medical technology, and biotechnology, all enjoying accelerated growth, are just a few aspects of the numerous disciplines of science and study—and their benefits are immense and widely spread.

Let's go ahead and identify some of the advantages it brings, as we elaborate on how technology has assisted people through advances benefitting our personal lives, as well as various fields of practice.

Communication and Convenience

From hand-held computers to smartphones, technological advancements in the field of communication are mind-boggling and seemingly never-ending. The means and the modes of communication are virtually unlimited. Clarity of audio and digital transmission, speed and ease of service, and the relationship between proximity of goods and access to widespread distribution networks are some of the benefits of technological breakthrough in this field. Time is no longer such a constraint in communication and neither is cost.

As a society we are experiencing a wave of technology in almost all facets of our daily life, from our shopping habits, banking transactions, and the way we make travel arrangements, to how we enroll in academic institutions. We can certainly agree that technology has reduced errors in ordinary and repetitious tasks, saving us time and money.

Megapixel images and video, along with high fidelity audio systems, bring remarkable lucidity in ways never before experienced; certainly, an ideal feast for eyes and ears that are never satisfied with what they see and hear! Spreading information, broadcasting news, or sharing knowledge, technology has made it faster (flashed around the world in just milliseconds), easier, and, in selected ways, better!

Communication through technology has made it possible for our planet to become a tinier place. We can find and communicate with long-lost relatives/friends more easily and at an affordable rate. Furthermore, in order to offer Internet access to the remotest places on Earth, Google is sending balloons into the stratosphere, a layer which begins at about 33,000 feet above sea level. At an altitude of approximately 63,000 feet, the Internet-beaming antennas could get the entire planet online, as the first step toward creating what it calls a "network in the sky" and eventually bring "balloon-powered Internet" where no one would be left out.[50]

Convenience is one of the most evident benefits; new devices and systems provide a great deal of accessibility and accelerate personal and business transactions such as spending, banking, or just paying bills. Marketing can be accomplished by placing ads that reach millions of ready buyers on the Internet or through social networking sites. And what about *speed*? Another enormous advantage! From sending flowers to making payments, everything gets accomplished with just a few clicks or taps.

Unquestionably, technology has evolved and transformed our lives and society. Globally, it has brought tremendous growth and amazing value to the nations of our world. Used with discretion and in a constructive manner, it could have indisputably wonderful outcomes!

Business

Technology is undeniably an integral part of any *business*, right from the acquisition of computers and software to the implementation of networks and security tools. Business organizations can remain up-to-date and drive their sales and service initiatives forward, while new technologies help them survive and sustain competition and become more profitable. With the help of countless advanced technologies and new equipment, often the outcomes have been greater efficiencies and a correlating fall in production costs.

Such growths in productivity go hand-in-hand with other efficiencies, too, such as improved speed, the ease of sharing and storing information, and a decrease in human error through new processes of automation. These bring about a reduction in costs and an increase in revenue.

Because they are more swift and agile, small businesses may compete with larger ones. They can respond to change faster than larger businesses. Today, information technology has significantly leveled the playing field, allowing the sharing of information and data at an unprecedented rate, saving time, and enabling important decisions to be made more quickly.

On-site training via e-learning and other forms of online education have reshaped the readiness of the average small business workforce, as employees can listen to classroom lectures and share ideas with classmates from the comfort of their home or office. This eliminates the need for small enterprises to hire training staff or face the costs and inconvenience of down-time while employees attend teaching courses in remote locations.

Technology allows small endeavors to automate certain functions that in the past would have required hiring an employee. For instance, bookkeeping functions can now be handled by software applications, and the sales function can be automated through contact management sites. This gives the small business owner the ability to focus on strategy and cut down on labor expenses.

Company accounts and customer records are easily stored and accessed, and this increases the market infiltration of any business. Global collaborations and partnerships are easier to start and maintain, much to the benefit of everyone involved in worldwide business. The same data-management tools also eliminate the need for double or triple entry systems and reduce the need to file large amounts of paperwork. Now, contracts and customer information can be stored in virtual data warehouses and accessed in minutes, which cuts down on the need to purchase or rent storage space.

Education

Today, e-learning is a familiar and popular term. A benefit of technology in this field is the *personalized training experience*, one where learners are able to take control and manage their own study. They set their own goals, manage the process and content of learning, and communicate with peers. Another benefit is *immediate response*, one where most e-learning programs provide immediate feedback on trainee assessments. Similarly, there are features such as chat, discussion boards, e-libraries, etc., that allow clarification at a faster speed than in traditional classrooms. A third advantage is that it is *self-paced,* enabling learners to chart courses at their own pace. This ensures higher levels of motivation both in terms of completing the course as well as in performance. And finally a *greater access,* which is where *technological advancements* have opened education to students with learning disabilities.

Distance study has become much easier, leading to a rise in the number of people who receive a comprehensive education. Universities are offering online degree programs, making higher education available to those whose schedules otherwise would not have allowed them to advance.

Satellite technology is also used to teach people in isolated communities, offering high-quality education and opportunities for future career development. The use of computers in classrooms and homes have opened up a whole new method of teaching and effective learning.

Healthcare

When we venture into the *healthcare* pool, the communication factor between patients and doctors has become less formal, more personal and flexible, and conducted with greater sensitivity, while medical research has led to the reduction or eradication of many diseases and ailments. Confidential records of patients are easily digitized and preserved electronically, making it easier for researchers to filter out symptoms of thousands of patients, study them and come up with new diagnoses and treatments for previously inexplicable conditions.

Physicians can also now follow up, provide advice, and re-direct patients to resources on the Internet. This saves time and reduces office visits. Medical aids have helped patients overcome many health conditions that they had to live with earlier; and therapeutic devices allow patients to complete their recovery at home, thus reducing the length of their hospital stay.

Medical technology supports the very young, the elderly, and patients with complex birth defects, chronic illnesses, and disabilities by alleviating their problems so that they can enjoy the most favorable lifestyle possible.

Numerous applications have been written and designed for people with special needs, and professionals claim that tablet computers and selected games can improve everything from fine motor skills to socialization with peers.

Parents of children with autism spectrum disorder are finding a host of uses for smartphones, iPads and Leap Pads. Some applications help them to improve their academic skills in subjects such as math and reading. Other apps are focused on assisting with specific problems that individuals with autistic disorders face, such as communication, motor and cognitive skills issues.

Religion

Because so many people have easy and ongoing access to the World Wide Web in everyday life—from banking to shopping to socializing—it is not surprising that *religious organizations* are seizing the opportunity and migrating their churches and temples to virtual real estate in order to stay relevant and to be online—where the people are!

Faith community leaders have websites, blogs and Twitter feeds; there are email prayer lines and online doctrinal studies; and there are social networks and apps that call the faithful to prayer. Being web-savvy today is a required skill for spiritual guides in general.

Social networks, including Facebook, have active and

closely-knit communities of religious followers of all doctrines. The web is overindulged with "sacred" spaces and, if anything, God has been disengaged from traditional doctrine to become everything to everybody. This has an upside as well as a downside. But, that's completely another subject.

Unsurprisingly, this has affected how organized religion engages with the new "mission field." Evangelicals, who have historically been intense in getting their message out via whatever communication conduit available, were the first organized religious groups to embrace the web. Non-traditional or sidelined spiritual movements quickly followed and made early moves online as well to get their version out.

What has traditionally been behind closed doors in ecclesiastical councils is now online, challenging the control that leaders once held over doctrine and their flocks. Just as the Reformation was ushered in by the printing press in the sixteenth century,[51] allowing people to access the texts for themselves and distribute their views freely and widely, the web has helped proliferate different interpretations and articulations of religions, and so we have witnessed the arrival of new faith communities.

Individuals now have a much more autonomous role in deciding whom to approach as a source. Those people may have official, traditional credentials, or they may even be Reverend Google.

Seniors
Technology has come a long way over the course of the lifetime of many older adults. *Seniors and their caregivers* have witnessed everything from the first successful optical or light laser to dramatic medical advances and the rise of an Internet-dependent society.

Seniors also bear witness to the ways technology is changing the face of aging, and impacting their quality of life by providing solutions that may help to keep them, as older adults, healthy, safe and socially connected while making caregiving tasks less stressful for their family members.

Staying socially engaged is just as important to healthy aging as genetic factors and maintaining an active body. While no technology can take the place of in-person human interaction, video chat services like Skype, or Internet-based communication channels such as email and social media can supplement seniors' social contacts when visits with friends and family aren't possible or are too infrequent.

Surveys consistently show that 80 to 90 percent of seniors want to stay in their own home as they age. A number of technological solutions can make doing so safer for them. Any senior who lives alone may now have a Personal Emergency Response System (PERS) that they wear on their body. A PERS device allows the aged person to call for help with the simple push of a button. We have all seen the popular TV commercial, "I've fallen and I can't get up."[52] Both seniors and their families can have peace of mind knowing that it can facilitate a call for help in any emergency situation.

Safety is also a major concern for seniors who suffer from Alzheimer's disease or other dementias, especially individuals who may be prone to wandering. A number of GPS tracking devices that can monitor a senior's location and send alerts are great tools to keep caregivers' worries at bay and prevent potentially dangerous or life-threatening situations.

Nursing homes and assisted living communities have already recognized the recreational and exercise benefits that certain video games deliver for elderly adults. Seniors living at home may also benefit by owning a video game system involving the use of motor skills. This enjoyable form of therapy offers an entertaining opportunity for them to engage in light physical activity from the comfort and safety of their own living room. Likewise, for mental exercise, the elderly are able to participate in games that include spatial recognition, fact recall, or memory and matching.

A recent study[53] at the University of California, Los Angeles, (UCLA), showed that older people who had prior familiarity with searching online, had a much greater degree of mind activation when they surfed the Internet. That activity was measured on a Magnetic Resonance Imaging (MRI) scanner and compared to those who had little experience using the Internet. The point is this: *they're exercising their brains* when they're searching online. There is a lot of activity in the front part of the head (the frontal lobe). That is considered the thinking brain, and the part of the brain that makes decisions. So when they search online, they're making lots of choices. They are constantly asking questions such as, "Should I go to this website?" "Should I go to that one, or maybe I should stay here a little longer?"

Many seniors find it challenging to keep track of their medications. Pillboxes can help, but technological solutions that also provide "time to refill" alerts potentially assist them in keeping to the prescribed medication schedule. The elderly and their custodians may now take advantage of smartphone reminder apps to reduce incidences of missed medications and to prevent medication errors. Such smartphone apps and cloud-based health information tracking systems now help seniors and their family caregivers keep information organized and handy — including medical history, physician contact details, medication schedules, and specifics of present health conditions. Tracking tools also make it much easier for healthcare professionals to have access to a complete set of information about their senior patients, thus helping make the most informed treatment decisions.

Smartphone and tablet applications that are used in managing Parkinson's disease (PD) range from simple medication reminders to logging and accurately reporting warning signs to a patient's healthcare team. One of the concepts where technology is used in PD treatment is cueing to manage symptoms. Signaling the brain with an auditory or visual reminder can help patients reduce their symptoms, especially freezing episodes and a shuffling gait.

So, we can see the immense benefits that technology has brought to many aspects of our lives, making them easier and better. But we must be on alert that, while we are reaping the benefits of modern technology, we are not also losing ourselves in it as well. Guard your mind...

~

"Above all else, guard your heart,
for everything you do flows from it."

—Proverbs of King Solomon 4:23 (NIV)

~

EPILOGUE

TAKING THE PLEDGE

Unplugging,
When It's the Right Thing to Do

The fact of the matter is that lots of digital natives and some digital immigrants need a digital detox!

- We tweet while we drive;
- We scroll while we walk;
- We text while we talk;
- We surf while we fall asleep;
- We are plugged in day and night, and we are expected to be available 24/7.

Without doubt, our lives and careers spin around the Internet in a vortex comprised of a mixture of technological gadgets.

So, here are some practical ways of how we can disconnect and, in return, concentrate on others rather than just on ourselves.

As a first step, it is very important to find out which group you and I find ourselves in.

- If you are generous (noble), it will be a gentle drive;
- If you are materialistic (selfish), it will be a somewhat bumpy ride but you will get there.

So let's start by selecting the time span of your preference:

A day a week without access to or use of the Internet
Are you already panicking? Then start with a less drastic approach.

A half-day a week without access to or use of the Internet
Now, turn ALL devices off and take a look around, just the two of you: YOURSELF and YOUR PROSPECT FOR FREEDOM.

So, what is this freedom that we are referring to? It is the *independence* that you do not fully have today. It is the ability to make a noble decision! So let's together shift from the automaton mode to the human being mode!

Here are seven suggestions that will help as you start your journey:

- Do something respectable intentionally
- Explore the beauty of nature
- Be kind to someone you dislike
- Compliment a stranger
- Forgive someone that did you wrong
- Share a meal with a neighbor
- Help somebody that is in need

A one-week fast
A weekly fast in which we avoid the use of technology will refresh and rejuvenate our minds and, in order to step off this wheel of endless sameness, this premeditated *inactivity* will allow us to accomplish it. It's a ritual that pushes us out of the norm, makes us pursue different projects, and causes us to use specific parts of our brain. This particular exercise provides the motivation to unplug our wired intelligence from the matrix of cyberspace so that we may explore the joy of real life.

Fasting is an intentional, periodic break from the Internet, e-mail, Facebook, Twitter, Pinterest, and Instagram, as well as the devices that deliver all these and more into each of our brains.

What are some of the benefits of fasting?

- First, it helps us to set time aside for more relaxation, but more than that, it allows for an opportunity to attend to a more enriching recreational experience, from "quantity time" (that was not a typo—it means "more" time) with family members and friends to extended sessions of reading, writing, and/or meditation.
- Second, fasting alleviates the over-stimulation and stress that come with any electronic engagement.
- And finally, unplugging helps us to restore and/or increase our ability to think, analyze, and process long-form material and complicated projects.

Upon undertaking this fast, you might discover things about yourself (or what you have inadvertently become), that you weren't consciously aware of. Some of the things unpluggers discovered, according to Jessica Hullinger[54], were:

- We are addicted to information;
- We share too much;
- We are addicted to ourselves;
- We need more downtime;

Might this be you?

When we take a Tech Sabbath, we cease from being plugged in and can spend time taking pleasure in and appreciating the magnificent things around us—whether it be enjoying such things as our friendships, our children, a crusty loaf of bread we baked ourselves, the inventions of mankind, art, wine, books — or the astonishing, live world that awaits outside our door. It's also a chance to reflect upon and appreciate the technology from which we are resting; a Tech Sabbath can serve as a reminder that what can feel like a burden is truly an amazing tool if controlled and used properly.

There are always incredible moments waiting to be discovered, but they won't be found in a social media network. They are hidden in plain sight among the people, places, food, and culture of wherever we find ourselves in the real world.

So, why not make a conscious decision to enjoy this life's journey as you consciously work towards "un-hacking your mind!"

GLOSSARY OF TERMS

CBT	Cognitive Behavioral Therapy
DNA	Deoxyribonucleic acid
DNS	Domain Name System
EMP	Electromagnetic Pulse
FOMO	Fear of missing out
GPS	Global Positioning Systems
GSM	Global System for Mobile Communications
IMSI	International Mobile Subscriber Identity
IP	Internet Protocol
IRL	In Real Life
ISP	Internet Service Provider
ITS	Intelligent Transportation System
MAC	Media Access Control
MORIS	Mobile Offender Recognition & Information System
MP4	Media Player
MRI	Magnetic Resonance Imaging
NFC	Near field communication
NSA	National Security Agency
OCD	Obsessive–compulsive disorder
PCB	Printed Circuit Board
PD	Parkinson's Disease
PERS	Personal Emergency Response System
RAND	Research And Development
RFID	Radio-frequency identification
TSA	Transportation Security Administration
UAV	Unmanned Aerial Vehicle
URL	Uniform Resource Locator

ABOUT THE AUTHOR

Jorge Rudko was born at the advent of the computer age, before the widespread adoption of digital technology, and was nurtured alongside the rise of the cyber culture movement.

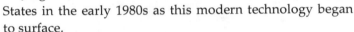

An Argentinean native, he grew up in the city of Buenos Aires to parents that emigrated from the Ukraine.

Jorge moved to the United States in the early 1980s as this modern technology began to surface.

Interestingly, he worked for a multinational telecommunications company, often holding the position of regional top trader, when cellphones were just becoming the "must have" novelty.

Jorge also worked professionally in various capacities for the Spanish news network of the National Broadcasting Company.

He has served in the Argentinean army and continues to serve his fellow men, with the same pride in country and culture, whether it be the United States, or Argentina.

Jorge is currently an education specialist in the North Carolina Area Health Education Center, where he is involved in the area of Public Health. His duties broaden as a consecutive and simultaneous interpreter and a certified medical interpreters' trainer.

Jorge is also an ordained minister, a certified premarital and marriage prepare-enrich professional. As a qualified

Crown associate, he teaches family finances.

Jorge and his beautiful wife, Adrianne—"the best cook in the world"—live in Charlotte, North Carolina. They have four wonderful sons—Jeremy, Steven, David and Michael, plus the added blessing of two beautiful daughters-in-law, Lindsey and Oksana, and four adorable grandchildren—Scarlett, Jakobi, Azariah and Solomon, who fill their lives with added joy.

You may contact Jorge by visiting his website at:

www.jorgerudko.com

ENDNOTES

[1] Jennifer Dutcher, *"What is Big Data?"* [September 03, 2014]. Accessed June 12, 2016. Berkeley,
https://datascience.berkeley.edu/what-is-big data/#JohnAkred

[2] Marshall 'Soulful' Jones, *"A 'Siirbaz' and his poem 'Touchscreen'"* Henry Brothers. [March 6, 2012]. Accessed March 8, 2016.
https://thehenrybrothers.wordpress.com/2012/03/06/marshall-soulfuljones-a-siirbaz-and-his-poem-touchscreen/

[3] Deborah Netburn, *"Facebook, Twitter, other social media are brain candy, study says"* Los Angeles Times [May 08, 2012] Accessed March 8, 2016.
http://articles.latimes.com/2012/may/08/business/la-fi-tn-self-disclosure-study-20120508

[4] Kendra Cherry, *"What is a Synapse"* [May 6, 2016]. Accessed June 12, 2016. verywell, https://www.verywell.com/what-is-a-synapse-2795867

[5] Robert M. Pirsig, *"Robert M. Pirsig Quotes"* 23rd quote. Notable Quotes, [n.d.]. Accessed March 8, 2016. http://www.notable-quotes.com/p/pirsig_robert_m.html

[6] Gary Small, *"Techno Addicts"* [July 22, 2009]. Accessed May 28, 2016. Psychology Today,
https://www.psychologytoday.com/blog/brain-bootcamp/200907/techno-addicts

[7] Larry Kim, *"Multitasking Is Killing Your Brain"* [February 2, 2016]. Accessed May 28, 2016. Observer Business & Tech,
http://observer.com/2016/02/multitasking-is-killing-your-brain/

[8] Alexandra Sifferlin, *"Why Facebook Makes You Feel Bad About Yourself"*, Time, New York, NY [Jan. 24, 2013]. Accessed March 8, 2016 http://www.healthland.time.com/2013/01/24/why-facebook-makes-you-feel-bad-about-yourself/

[9] Linda Sapadin, *"Fear of Missing Out"* Psych Central Newburyport, MA [2015]. Accessed March 8, 2016
http://www.psychcentral.com/blog/archives/2015/10/12/fear-of-missing-out/

[10] Eric Oster, *"'Phubbing' is Still a Thing According to McCann Melbourne, Macquarie Dictionary"* Agency Spy New York City, NY [October 14, 2013]. Accessed August 10, 2016 http://www.adweek.com/agencyspy/phubbing-is-still-a-thing-according-to-mccann-melbourne-macquarie-dictionary/55831

[11] University of Southern California Marshall School of Business, *"Media consumption to average 15.5 hours a day by 2015."* [October 30, 2013]. Accessed June 22, 2016. ScienceDaily, https://www.sciencedaily.com/releases/2013/10/131030111316.htm

[12] Susan Weinschenk, *"Why We're All Addicted to Texts, Twitter and Google",* Psychology Today, New York, NY [Sep. 11, 2012]. Accessed June 7, 2016 https://www.psychologytoday.com/blog/brain-wise/201209/why-were-all-addicted-texts-twitter-and-google

[13] Fear of being without one's phone; see http://www.scientificamerican.com/article/scientists-study-nomophobia-mdash-fear-of-being-without-a-mobile-phone/

[14] http://www.beliefnet.com/columnists/idolchatter/2010/06/this-is-your-brain-on-technolo.html#

[15] Natalie Wolchover, *"What Is Internet Use Disorder?"* [October 04, 2012]. Accessed March 8, 2016. Livescience, http://www.livescience.com/34264-internet-use-disorder-addiction.html

[16] WIP, *"What Is Stockholm Syndrome?"* [February 21, 2012]. Accessed June 7, 2016. What is Psychology? http://www.whatispsychology.biz/what-stockholm-syndrome-definition

[17] Mayo Clinic Staff, *"Cognitive behavioral therapy"* Mayo Clinic [February 23, 2016]. Accessed March 8, 2016 http://www.mayoclinic.org/tests-procedures/cognitive-behavioral-therapy/basics/definition/prc-20013594

[18] Jeff DeGraff, *"Digital Natives vs. Digital Immigrants?"* Huffpost Business, [Sep. 07, 2014]. Accessed June 7, 2016. http://www.huffingtonpost.com/jeff-degraff/digital-natives-vs-digita_b_5499606.html

[19] Judy Lin, *"Research shows that Internet is rewiring our brains"* UCLA Newsroom, [October 15, 2008]. Accessed June 22, 2016. http://newsroom.ucla.edu/stories/081015_gary-small-ibrain

[20] Merriam-Webster, *"Definition of Information Age"* [n.d.]. Accessed July 3, 2016. http://www.merriam-webster.com/dictionary/Information%20Age

[21] Andi Horvath, *"How does technology affect our brains?"* The Age, [June 4, 2015]. Accessed June 12, 2016. http://www.theage.com.au/national/education/voice/how-does-technology-affect-our-brains-20150604-3x5uq.html

[22] PC, *"Definition of E-ZPass"* Accessed June 22, 2016. http://www.pcmag.com/encyclopedia/term/68406/e-zpass

[23] Library of Congress, *"United States: Gun Ownership and the Supreme Court"*, [n.d.]. Accessed June 12, 2016. https://www.loc.gov/law/help/second-amendment.php

[24] The Economist, *"What caused the flash crash?* [October 1, 2010]. Accessed June 22, 2016. http://www.economist.com/blogs/newsbook/2010/10/what_caused_flash_crash

[25] Tana Ganeva, *"Why is the Government Collecting Your Biometric Data?"* Alternet, San Fransisco, CA [June 23, 2012]. Accessed March 26, 2016. http://www.alternet.org/story/155939/why_is_the_government_collecting_your_biometric_data

[26] Whatis.com, *"Digital Footprint"* [n.d.]. Accessed July 3, 2016. http://whatis.techtarget.com/definition/digital-footprint

[27] James Cook, *"Everything We Know About The Mysterious Fake Cell Towers Across the US That Could Be Tapping Your Phone"* Business Insider, [Sep. 22, 2014]. Accessed June 12, 2016. http://www.businessinsider.com/mysterious-fake-cellphone-towers-2014-9

[28] Clarence Walker, *"New Hi-Tech Police Surveillance: The "Sting-Ray"* Cell Phone Spying Device" Global Research, Quebec, CA [May 19, 2015]. Accessed March 8, 2016. http://www.globalresearch.ca/new-hi-tech-police-surveillance-the-stingray-cell-phone-spying-device/5331165

[29] United States Courts, *"What Does the Fourth Amendment Mean?"* [n.d.] Accessed March 8, 2016.
http://www.uscourts.gov/educational-resources/get-involved/constitution-activities/fourth-amendment/fourth-amendment-mean.aspx

[30] Ron Nixon, *"TSA Expands Duties Beyond Airport Security"*. The New York Times. [August 5, 2013]. Accessed March 8, 2016.
http://www.nytimes.com/2013/08/06/us/tsa-expands-duties-beyond-airportsecurity.html?pagewanted=all&_r=0

[31] Misha Glenny, *"Who controls the internet"* FT Magazine UK [October 8, 2010] Accessed June 12, 2016.
http://www.ft.com/cms/s/2/3e52897c-d0ee-11df-a426-00144feabdc0.html

[32] Peter Kelly-Detwiler, *"Failure to Protect U.S. Against Electromagnetic Pulse Threat Could Make 9/11 Look Trivial Someday"* Forbes, [July 31, 2014] Accessed August 6, 2016.
http://www.forbes.com/sites/peterdetwiler/2014/07/31/protecting-the-u-s-against-the-electromagnetic-pulse-threat-a-continued-failure-of-leadership-could-make-911-look-trivial-someday/#5b918a097fcd

[33] Kai Ekholm & Paivikki Karhula, *"Sleepwalking toward a control society? Ten Must-Know Trends"* IFLA, Netherlands [August 2, 2013] Accessed June 12, 2016.
http://www.ifla.org/files/assets/faife/publications/spotlights/sleepwalking-ekholm-karhula.pdf

[34] Mark Millan, *"Digital photos can reveal your location, raise privacy fears"*, *CNN*, Atlanta, GA [October 15, 2010] Accessed August 10, 2016.
http://www.cnn.com/2010/TECH/web/10/15/photo.gps.privacy/

[35] Miguel Helft and Tanzina Vega, *"Retargeting Ads Follow Surfers to Other Sites"*, *The New York Times*, New York City, NY [August 29, 2010] Accessed August 10, 2016.
http://www.nytimes.com/2010/08/30/technology/30adstalk.html?_r=0

[36] *US Constitution, "US Constitution – 5th and 14th Amendments"* findUSlaw, [n.d.] Accessed August 7, 2016.
http://finduslaw.com/us-constitution-5th-14th-amendments

[37] Pao L. Chang, *"How Mnemonic is Used to Program and Control Your Mind"* Waking Times, [January 29, 2016] Accessed August 7, 2016. http://www.wakingtimes.com/2016/01/29/mnemonics-and-mind-control/

[38] Heather Callaghan, *"How TV Affects Your Brain Chemistry for the Worse"* The Mind Unleashed, [August 19, 2015] Accessed August 20, 2016. http://themindunleashed.org/2015/08/how-tv-affects-your-brain-chemistry-for-the-worse.html

[39] Remi Melina, *"What's the Difference Between the Right Brain and Left Brain?"* Live Science, [January 12, 2011] Accessed August 22, 2016. http://www.livescience.com/32935-whats-the-difference-between-the-right-brain-and-left-brain.html

[40] Tom Scheve, *"What's are endorphins?"* HowStuffWorks Science, [n.d.] Accessed August 22, 2016.
http://science.howstuffworks.com/life/endorphins.htm

[41] Regina Bailey, *"Limbic System"* about, Inc. [April 23, 2016] Accessed August 22, 2016.
http://biology.about.com/od/anatomy/a/aa042205a.htm

[42] Academic Earth, *"How the Internet is Changing Your Brain"*. Houston, TX [2009]. Accessed June 22, 2016.
http://academicearth.org/electives/internet-changing-your-brain/

[43] Christopher Bergland, *"Cortisol: Why "The Stress Hormone" Is Public Enemy No. 1"* Psychology Today. [January 22, 2013] Accessed August 22, 2016.
https://www.psychologytoday.com/blog/the-athletes-way/201301/cortisol-why-the-stress-hormone-is-public-enemy-no-1

[44] Steven D. Ehrlich, *"Melatolin"* University of Maryland Medical Center [February 3, 2016] Accessed August 22, 2016.
http://biology.about.com/od/anatomy/a/aa042205a.htm

[45] Merriam-Webster, *"Definition of brainwashing"* Springfield, MA [n.d.] Accessed June 24, 2016. http://www.merriam-webster.com/dictionary/brainwashing

[46] eMarketer, *"2 Billion Consumers Worldwide to Get Smart(phones) by 2016"*. New York, NY [December 11, 2014]. Accessed March 8, 2016. http://www.emarketer.com/Article/2-Billion-Consumers-Worldwide-Smartphones-by-2016/1011694

[47] Ecclesiastes 1:8, New International Version

[48] Bryan Kolb, Robbin Gibb, and Terry Robinson "Brain Plasticity and Behavior" Canadian Centre for Behavioural Neuroscience, University of Lethbridge, Alberta, Canada (B.K., RG.), and Department of Psychology, University of Michigan, Ann Arbor, Michigan (T.R.) [n.d.]. Accessed March 8, 2016.
www.psychologicalscience.org/journals/cd/12_1/Kolb.cfm

[49] History.com Staff, "Industrial Revolution" A+E Networks. [2009]. Accessed March 8, 2016. www.history.com/topics/industrial-revolution

[50] Google+ *"Project Loon"* [n.d.]. Viewed March 8, 2016
https://plus.google.com/+ProjectLoon/posts

[51] www.history.com/topics/reformation

[52] You Tube, *"I've Fallen and I Can't Get Up"* Life Alarm [August 10, 2007] Accessed June 12, 2016.
https://www.youtube.com/watch?v=bQlpDiXPZHQ

[53] Rachel Champeau, *"First-time Internet users find boost in brain function after just one week"* UCLA Los Angeles CA Newsroom | [October 19, 2009] Accessed March 8, 2016.
http://newsroom.ucla.edu/releases/first-time-internet-users-find-111275

[54] Jessica Hullinger, *"Stories From Beyond The Plug"*. New York, NY [June 27, 2013]. Accessed June 22, 2016.
http://www.fastcompany.com/3013555/unplug/stories-from-beyond-the-plug